教育部"拓金计划"建设成果
"上海高校一流本科课程"建设成果
"上海高校市级重点课程"建设成果
"全国高校外语教学科研项目"建设成果
"上海高校优青科研专项基金"建设成果
"文心译道课程思政名师工作室"建设成果

New Academic Translation Practice

主 编 ◎ 郑 晶

新编学术翻译实务

副主编 ◎ 康添俊　范懿明

参　编 ◎ 金晓冬　魏　兰　李雪彦
　　　　　张伟香　葛晓燕　唐思文

同济大学出版社
TONGJI UNIVERSITY PRESS
·上海·

图书在版编目(CIP)数据

新编学术翻译实务 / 郑晶主编. -- 上海：同济大学出版社,2022.6(2025.7重印)
ISBN 978-7-5765-0279-4

Ⅰ.①新… Ⅱ.①郑… Ⅲ.①学术－英语－翻译－教材 Ⅳ.①H315.9

中国版本图书馆 CIP 数据核字(2022)第 113046 号

新编学术翻译实务
郑　晶　主编

| 出 品 人 | 金英伟 | 策　划 | 赵俊丽 | 责任编辑 | 王红菠 |
| 责任校对 | 徐春莲 | 封面设计 | 渲彩轩 | | |

出版发行　同济大学出版社　www.tongjipress.com.cn
　　　　　(地址：上海市四平路1239号　邮编：200092　电话：021-65985622)
经　　销　全国各地新华书店
制　　作　南京月叶图文制作有限公司
印　　刷　启东市人民印刷有限公司
开　　本　787mm×1092mm　1/16
印　　张　10.75
字　　数　235 000
版　　次　2022年6月第1版
印　　次　2025年7月第3次印刷
书　　号　ISBN 978-7-5765-0279-4

定　　价　42.00元

本书若有印装质量问题,请向本社发行部调换　　版权所有　侵权必究

前　言

近年来,随着教育技术的发展和教学理念的更新,线上线下混合式教学模式不断发展,从理论原型建构到教学实践落地,混合式教学成为不少高校主推的教学新模态。新的教学模式呼吁新形态教材与之相契合。从选材角度来看,翻译教材主要分为两大类:一是文学类翻译教材,主要面向英语专业学生,所选材料偏重文学;二是科技类翻译教材,主要面向理工类高年级本科生或者研究生,所选材料专业性强,属于专业英语教学范畴。目前市场上的翻译教材大都为传统型教材,即以书面材料为主,开展技巧讲解和翻译实践。因此,编写一本新形态的通用型学术翻译教材既是来自一线教师的呼声,也是金课建设的重要课题。

在这样的背景下,笔者基于十余年翻译教学的积淀和近年来线上线下混合式课程建设的经验,精心打造了新形态翻译教材《新编学术翻译实务》。本教材是上海高校一流本科课程、上海高校市级重点课程、教育部"拓金计划"、全国高校外语教学科研项目、上海高校选拔培养优秀青年教师科研专项基金项目、校级重点课程、校级线上线下混合式示范课程、校级课程思政领航课程等的建设成果,也是多年来笔者一系列翻译教材建设中的最新成果。笔者从最初的校印讲义开始,先后作为第一主编出版教材7册,作为第二主编或副主编出版教材4册,全力服务翻译教学。

本教材采用"新形态教材"的编写体例,是一本为混合式教学量身打造的翻译教材,不仅适合学生线上自主建构知识,而且适合教师线下开展面授辅导,助力广大师生开展线上线下混合式翻译教学。教材内容紧密围绕"香精香料化妆品和绿色化工""功能新材料和智能制造""设计与文创"三大特色学科专业群,含"经济管理""语言文化""社会研究""法律法规""文创设计""生化工程""电子技术""智能制造""土木建筑""香精香料"十个单元。附录部分提供了全国大学英语四、六级考试翻译考题(汉译英)指南,全国研究生入学考试翻译考题(英译汉)指南和口译加油站。每个教学单元及附录均提供笔者设计录制的教学视频,包括学科背景、笔译技巧、口译技巧、实例剖析、四六级翻译辅导和考研翻译辅导等，内容丰富，层次鲜明。

　　本教材定位为通用学术英语教学，主要服务各专业本科生及低年级研究生。总体而言，本教材注重学术翻译的基础性教学，包括翻译技巧讲授、学术翻译实践和高阶思辨训练，助力广大学子的专业发展；为学生提供高校阶段权威英语考试翻译考题的题型、题源、难点、策略等信息，帮助学生在相关考试中得心应手，顺利过关；同时，积极向上的选材内容也有益于提升学生的人文修养和学科素质，培养爱国情怀和敬业精神。更为重要的是，这本新形态教材采取开放式编写理念，动态融合金课建设的最新成果，日后将陆续补充各类有益的教学视频和线上资源，不断改进，不断完善。

　　正值《新编学术翻译实务》出版之际，笔者愿借此机会，感谢多方给予的支持与帮助。

　　首先，感谢教育部和上海市教委为积极推进课程建设和教学大赛所做出的努力，为广大一线教师搭建了一个相互切磋与共同提高的平台！

　　其次，感谢每一位参与编写工作的教师和参与审阅工作的编辑，教材的顺利出版离不开你们的认真负责和辛勤付出，诚挚感谢你们的鼎力相助！

　　再次，感谢使用本教材的广大师生和翻译爱好者，希望能够多多收到你们的使用反馈和宝贵建议，你们的信任和支持是我们永不枯竭的动力！

　　最后，感谢我的家人，忙碌时刻，你们的理解令我欣慰；艰难岁月，你们的宽慰让我释怀；收获季节，你们的鼓励教会我不骄不躁、勇于前行！

主编　郑　晶
2022 年 6 月

Contents
目　录

Chapter 1　Economy & Management　经济管理 ················· 1
　Ⅰ. Academic Background 学术背景汇报 ················· 1
　Ⅱ. E-C Academic Translation 英汉学术翻译 ················· 1
　　　Post-globalization Era ················· 2
　Ⅲ. C-E Academic Translation 汉英学术翻译 ················· 3
　　　大腕雇主七大法宝 ················· 5
　Ⅳ. Extended Terms and Expressions 词汇拓展训练 ················· 6
　Ⅴ. Sentence Translation 句子翻译训练 ················· 6
　Ⅵ. Abstract Translation 摘要翻译训练 ················· 8
　Ⅶ. Academic Debate 学术思辨训练 ················· 9
　Ⅷ. Theoretical Guidance 翻译理论指导 ················· 10
　　　笔译技巧:词性转换 ················· 10

Chapter 2　Language & Culture　语言文化 ················· 12
　Ⅰ. Academic Background 学术背景汇报 ················· 12
　Ⅱ. E-C Academic Translation 英汉学术翻译 ················· 12
　　　Vanishing Voices ················· 13
　Ⅲ. C-E Academic Translation 汉英学术翻译 ················· 14
　　　舶来语 ················· 14
　Ⅳ. Extended Terms and Expressions 词汇拓展训练 ················· 15
　Ⅴ. Sentence Translation 句子翻译训练 ················· 16
　Ⅵ. Abstract Translation 摘要翻译训练 ················· 18
　Ⅶ. Academic Debate 学术思辨训练 ················· 19
　Ⅷ. Theoretical Guidance 翻译理论指导 ················· 20
　　　笔译技巧:增词减词 ················· 20

Chapter 3　Sociological Studies　社会研究 ················· 22
　Ⅰ. Academic Background 学术背景汇报 ················· 22
　Ⅱ. E-C Academic Translation 英汉学术翻译 ················· 22

　　　　Pandemic ………………………………………………………… 23
　　Ⅲ. C-E Academic Translation 汉英学术翻译 ……………………… 24
　　　　人口普查 ………………………………………………………… 24
　　Ⅳ. Extended Terms and Expressions 词汇拓展训练 ……………… 25
　　Ⅴ. Sentence Translation 句子翻译训练 …………………………… 25
　　Ⅵ. Abstract Translation 摘要翻译训练 …………………………… 27
　　Ⅶ. Academic Debate 学术思辨训练 ……………………………… 28
　　Ⅷ. Theoretical Guidance 翻译理论指导 …………………………… 29
　　　　笔译技巧：分译合译 …………………………………………… 29

Chapter 4　Law & Regulation　法律法规 …………………………… 32
　　Ⅰ. Academic Background 学术背景汇报 ………………………… 32
　　Ⅱ. E-C Academic Translation 英汉学术翻译 ……………………… 32
　　　　Operational Mode of American Law Firms …………………… 33
　　Ⅲ. C-E Academic Translation 汉英学术翻译 ……………………… 33
　　　　保障法治营商环境建设 ………………………………………… 34
　　Ⅳ. Extended Terms and Expressions 词汇拓展训练 ……………… 35
　　Ⅴ. Sentence Translation 句子翻译训练 …………………………… 35
　　Ⅵ. Abstract Translation 摘要翻译训练 …………………………… 38
　　Ⅶ. Academic Debate 学术思辨训练 ……………………………… 38
　　Ⅷ. Theoretical Guidance 翻译理论指导 …………………………… 39
　　　　笔译技巧：语序转换 …………………………………………… 39

Chapter 5　Cultural & Creative Design　文创设计 ………………… 41
　　Ⅰ. Academic Background 学术背景汇报 ………………………… 41
　　Ⅱ. E-C Academic Translation 英汉学术翻译 ……………………… 41
　　　　Forever Barbie …………………………………………………… 42
　　Ⅲ. C-E Academic Translation 汉英学术翻译 ……………………… 43
　　　　设计中的文化元素 ……………………………………………… 44
　　Ⅳ. Extended Terms and Expressions 词汇拓展训练 ……………… 45
　　Ⅴ. Sentence Translation 句子翻译训练 …………………………… 46
　　Ⅵ. Abstract Translation 摘要翻译训练 …………………………… 47
　　Ⅶ. Academic Debate 学术思辨训练 ……………………………… 48
　　Ⅷ. Theoretical Guidance 翻译理论指导 …………………………… 49
　　　　笔译技巧：语态转换 …………………………………………… 49

Chapter 6　Biochemical Engineering　生化工程 ········· 51
　Ⅰ. Academic Background 学术背景汇报 ············· 51
　Ⅱ. E-C Academic Translation 英汉学术翻译 ········ 51
　　　Chemical Weapons — Sarin ··············· 52
　Ⅲ. C-E Academic Translation 汉英学术翻译 ········ 53
　　　原油分馏 ··························· 53
　Ⅳ. Extended Terms and Expressions 词汇拓展训练 ··· 54
　Ⅴ. Sentence Translation 句子翻译训练 ············ 54
　Ⅵ. Abstract Translation 摘要翻译训练 ············· 57
　Ⅶ. Academic Debate 学术思辨训练 ··············· 57
　Ⅷ. Theoretical Guidance 翻译理论指导 ············ 58
　　　口译技巧：应对策略 ····················· 58

Chapter 7　Electronic Technology　电子技术 ············ 60
　Ⅰ. Academic Background 学术背景汇报 ············· 60
　Ⅱ. E-C Academic Translation 英汉学术翻译 ········ 60
　　　Artificial Intelligence ················· 61
　Ⅲ. C-E Academic Translation 汉英学术翻译 ········ 62
　　　智能诈骗 ··························· 63
　Ⅳ. Extended Terms and Expressions 词汇拓展训练 ··· 63
　Ⅴ. Sentence Translation 句子翻译训练 ············ 64
　Ⅵ. Abstract Translation 摘要翻译训练 ············· 66
　Ⅶ. Academic Debate 学术思辨训练 ··············· 67
　Ⅷ. Theoretical Guidance 翻译理论指导 ············ 68
　　　口译技巧：记忆训练 ····················· 68

Chapter 8　Intelligent Manufacturing　智能制造 ········· 70
　Ⅰ. Academic Background 学术背景汇报 ············· 70
　Ⅱ. E-C Academic Translation 英汉学术翻译 ········ 70
　　　Revolution of Manufacturing ············· 71
　Ⅲ. C-E Academic Translation 汉英学术翻译 ········ 72
　　　自动化技术 ·························· 73
　Ⅳ. Extended Terms and Expressions 词汇拓展训练 ··· 73
　Ⅴ. Sentence Translation 句子翻译训练 ············ 74
　Ⅵ. Abstract Translation 摘要翻译训练 ············· 75

Ⅶ. Academic Debate 学术思辨训练 ……………………………………… 76
Ⅷ. Theoretical Guidance 翻译理论指导 …………………………………… 77
　　口译技巧：预测听辨 …………………………………………………… 77

Chapter 9　Civil Engineering & Architecture　土木建筑 ……………… 79
　Ⅰ. Academic Background 学术背景汇报 ………………………………… 79
　Ⅱ. E-C Academic Translation 英汉学术翻译 …………………………… 79
　　　Transparent Cement ………………………………………………… 80
　Ⅲ. C-E Academic Translation 汉英学术翻译 …………………………… 80
　　　建筑结构 ……………………………………………………………… 81
　Ⅳ. Extended Terms and Expressions 词汇拓展训练 …………………… 82
　Ⅴ. Sentence Translation 句子翻译训练 ………………………………… 83
　Ⅵ. Abstract Translation 摘要翻译训练 …………………………………… 85
　Ⅶ. Academic Debate 学术思辨训练 ……………………………………… 86
　Ⅷ. Theoretical Guidance 翻译理论指导 …………………………………… 87
　　　口译技巧：速记策略 ………………………………………………… 87

Chapter 10　Perfume & Aroma　香精香料 ………………………………… 89
　Ⅰ. Academic Background 学术背景汇报 ………………………………… 89
　Ⅱ. E-C Academic Translation 英汉学术翻译 …………………………… 89
　　　French Perfumes …………………………………………………… 90
　Ⅲ. C-E Academic Translation 汉英学术翻译 …………………………… 91
　　　香料的发展 …………………………………………………………… 91
　Ⅳ. Extended Terms and Expressions 词汇拓展训练 …………………… 92
　Ⅴ. Sentence Translation 句子翻译训练 ………………………………… 93
　Ⅵ. Abstract Translation 摘要翻译训练 …………………………………… 94
　Ⅶ. Academic Debate 学术思辨训练 ……………………………………… 95
　Ⅷ. Theoretical Guidance 翻译理论指导 …………………………………… 96
　　　口译技巧：处理数字 ………………………………………………… 96

附录1　全国大学英语四级考试翻译题型指南及真题演练 ………………… 98
附录2　全国大学英语六级考试翻译题型指南及真题演练 ………………… 101
附录3　全国研究生入学考试翻译考题指南及真题演练 …………………… 105
附录4　口译加油站 …………………………………………………………… 117

参考答案 …………………………………………………………………………… 122

Chapter 1　Economy & Management

经 济 管 理

Ⅰ. Academic Background 学术背景汇报

Directions: *Study the following questions before class and try to search for some relevant information. Then discuss these questions with your group members. Give a brief introduction to the discipline of economics and management and present it in class.*

1. What does the study of economics mainly cover?
2. Why do we need management?
3. Can you mention some major economic achievements enjoyed by China during the 21st century?
4. How do you understand cross-cultural management?

Ⅱ. E-C Academic Translation 英汉学术翻译

Directions: *Study the notes in advance, and then read the following passage carefully and translate it into Chinese with the help of the notes supplied. Try to enrich your academic vocabulary and sentence patterns.*

1. compound a shift from A to B　加速从A到B的转变
2. shrink　v. (使)收缩;(使)萎缩
3. stagnate　v. 停滞
4. sluggish　adj. 懒散的;无力的;反应迟缓的;萧条的
5. sluggishness　n. 缓慢,停滞
6. slowbalization　n. 全球化放缓
7. sprawl　n./v. 四肢伸开躺卧;杂乱延展;无计划扩张
8. eat sb. alive　彻底击败某人
9. bloc　n. 集团(有相似政治利益的国家或人)
10. source from　v. 从……获得;从……采购
11. intra-regional　adj. 区域内部的(intra- 在……内部, inter- 在……之间)
12. patchwork　n. (不同图案杂色布块的)拼缝物;拼布工艺
13. a fluid patchwork　流畅的拼接;灵活的体系/机制/结构
14. sphere of influence　势力范围
15. assert control over ...　加强对……的控制

16. continental *adj.* 欧洲大陆的（不包括英国和爱尔兰）；北美大陆的；大洲的
17. continental-sized markets 洲内市场
18. pauper *n.* 穷人；贫民
19. reap net benefits from ... 从……中获得净收益
20. trade one's way to riches 以交易致富
21. the Federal Reserve 美国联邦储备委员会，简称"美联储"（the Fed）
22. set the pulse for 掌握……的命脉；生死与夺
23. financial turbulence 金融动荡
24. last resort 终极手段；最后一招
25. lender of last resort 最后贷款人；最后的救星
26. renaissance *n.* 文艺复兴；（某一学科、艺术形式、现象等衰落后的）复兴
27. tax-dodging *n.* 逃税
28. mitigate *v.* 减轻，缓和
29. on offer 提供的；供使用的；待售的
30. predecessor *n.* 前身；前任
31. discontent *n.* 不满（的缘由）；*v.* 使不满；使不快 *adj.* 不安分的；不平的
32. feed the discontent 助长不满情绪

Post-globalization Era

Today's trade tensions are compounding a shift that has been under way since the financial crisis in 2008. Cross-border investment, trade, bank loans and supply chains have all been shrinking or stagnating relative to world GDP. Globalization has given way to a new era of sluggishness. Adapting a term coined by a Dutch writer, we call it "slowbalization".

Slowbalization has slowed from light speed to a snail's pace in the past decade for several reasons. The cost of moving goods has stopped falling. Multinational firms have found that global sprawl burns money and that local rivals often eat them alive. Activity is shifting towards services, which are harder to sell across borders: scissors can be exported in 20ft-containers, but hair stylists cannot.

The new economic pattern will work differently. Slowbalization will lead to closer links within regional blocs. Supply chains in North America, Europe and Asia are sourcing more from closer to home. In Asia and Europe, most trade is already intra-regional, and the share has risen. Last year, Asian firms made more foreign sales within Asia than in America. As global rules decay, a fluid patchwork of regional deals and spheres of influence is asserting control over trade and investment.

Fortunately, this need not be a disaster for living standards. Continental-sized markets are large enough to prosper. Some 1.2bn people have been lifted out of extreme poverty, and there is no reason to think that the proportion of paupers will rise again. Western consumers will continue to reap large net benefits from trade. In some cases, deeper integration will take place at a regional level than could have happened at a global one.

Yet slowbalization has two big disadvantages. First, it creates new difficulties. In the past ten years, most emerging countries were able to close some of the gap with developed ones. Now more will struggle to trade their way to riches. And there is a tension between a more regional trading pattern and a global financial system in which Wall Street and the Federal Reserve set the pulse for markets everywhere. Most countries' interest rates will still be affected by America's even as their trade patterns become less linked to it, leading to financial turbulence. The Fed is less likely to rescue foreigners by acting as a global lender of last resort, as it did a decade ago.

Second, slowbalization will not fix the problems that globalization created. Automation means there will be no renaissance of blue-collar jobs in the West. Firms will hire unskilled workers in the cheapest places in each region. Climate change, migration and tax-dodging will be even harder to solve without global cooperation.

Slowbalization made the world a better place for almost everyone, but too little was done to mitigate its costs. The integrated world's neglected problems have now grown in the eyes of the public to the point where the benefits of the global order are easily forgotten. Yet the solution on offer is not really a fix at all. Slowbalization will be meaner and less stable than its predecessor. In the end it will only feed the discontent.

III. C-E Academic Translation 汉英学术翻译

Directions: *Study the notes in advance, and then read the following passage carefully and translate it into English with the help of the notes supplied. Try to enrich your academic vocabulary and sentence patterns.*

1. 令人不安的　unsettling; worrying
2. 费神的　energy-sapping; niggling
3. 令人遗憾的结果　a pitiful result; a sorry state of affairs
4. 无责任心的;自由散漫的　disengaged; idling around
5. 兢兢业业的;积极奋斗的　engaged; striving hard
6. 以绝对优势超过　exceed/outnumber/outstrip/overtake ... by an overwhelming ratio
7. 反(市场)潮流;抵制趋势　buck the trend
8. 破译秘诀　decode secret; crack a code
9. 服务业　service (industry/sector); hospitality industry
10. 总雇员人数达……　the number of

employees totals ...; the total amount of employees reaches ...; collectively employ ...

11. 惨淡而无望的　bleak and hopeless; gloomy and unpromising; bland and uninspiring

12. 起推动作用　promote; stimulate

13. 提高工作效率　increase working efficiency; improve efficiency of operations; lead to greater performance/productivity/efficiency of work

14. 良性循环　virtuous circle; beneficent cycle; positive succession

15. 恶性循环　vicious circle/cycle/spiral

16. 高谈阔论　talk with eloquence

17. 脚踏实地　stand on solid ground; stay grounded; be earnest and down-to-earth; do solid work

18. 出色地完成任务　fulfill a task excellently

19. 完全胜任　be good fits for ...; be perfectly competent for ...

20. 得到某人支持　have sb.'s backs; enjoy sb.'s support

21. 全身心地投入；致力于　commit to; be devoted to; devote oneself to

22. 拿……当借口　use ... as an excuse; find/seek a pretext; make an excuse for sth.; look for a get-out; do sth. with excuses

23. 下降；衰退；低迷时期　downturn; depression; slack time

24. 迅速转变　swiftly change; make changes swiftly; carry out immediate adjustments

25. 鼓舞士气　enhance/bolster/boost troop morale; encourage soldiers to keep up high morale; be a great morale booster; provide hope

26. 对……负责　be responsible for ...; hold accountable for ...

27. 打量；估计；判断　size up

28. 亲自做某事　do sth. in person; take a hands-on approach to do sth.

29. 特点；特征　characteristic; feature; hall-mark

30. 把……当作/看成……　see/regard/hold/look on ... as ...

31. 痛恨……　hate ...; see ... as the enemy

32. 关注　focus on sth.; keep one's eyes on sth.

33. 为之付出更高的投入　devote more to; need greater engagement

34. 体恤　understand and sympathize with; show solicitude for

35. 代表性样本研究　research into a representative sample

36. 大量的；充裕的；丰富的　copious; abundant; ample

37. 有趣的　fun; interesting; attractive

38. 时髦的　fashionable; funky; trendy

39. 有意义的　meaningful; significant

40. 无法如愿　be unable to do; fail (to do)

大腕雇主七大法宝

对于多数人而言,上班赚钱总是令人感到不安和极其费神。尽管雇员的投入度已经一跃成为首席执行官们优先考虑的重心,我们在全球各大行业开展的有关调查揭示了一个令人遗憾的结果:无责任心的员工以2:1的绝对优势远远超过了兢兢业业的雇员。所幸的是,确实有一些公司反其道而行之,而我们也已经破译了这些公司成功的秘诀。

经过5年的时间,我们研究了包括服务业、银行业、生产制造业、医院等七个领域的32家典型的公司(雇员总人数达60万人)。在这些公司中,积极奋斗的员工人数是自由散漫者的9倍。据我们所知,另有大批公司正在为改变惨淡而无望的工作现状苦苦挣扎。为了更好地了解少数公司占据显著优势的原因,我们针对两类企业开展对比研究。

我们发现雇员工作热情高涨的公司表现出以下七大特点,而这些显然正是其他众多公司的软肋所在。这七大因素都能带来高效与高产吗？无疑,至少其中某些因素促成了一种良性循环。我们坚信有必要积极推广这些秘诀,以敦促员工奋力工作:

1. 聘用拥有宏才大略、充满激情、不断前行的领导者。成功的业界领袖不会高谈阔论他们的远大理想,而是脚踏实地探索新型的管理模式,并每天带领自己的团队不断付诸实践,从而使管理更高效。

2. 首先确保具备最基本的工作条件,之后才能期待员工出色地完成任务。员工只有充分了解公司对自己的期待,具备完成任务所需的条件,能够胜任自己的角色,并感觉到上司是他们的坚强后盾,他们才能够全身心地致力于实现公司奋力赢取的目标。

3. 永远不要拿低迷期当借口。伴随着结构转型、生产过剩以及薪金和收益的减少,管理层往往无一例外,不得不应对公司业绩不景气甚至经济下滑等现象,因此需要通过解放理念、迅速调整、各方互通、鼓舞士气等手段来解决这一问题。

4. 信任队友,对团队负责,一如既往地支持团队成员。激励和鼓舞员工的做法是卓有成效、富有回报的。只有当团队成员能够携手共同剖析面对的问题并亲历亲为解决问题,我们才能够建立一个强大的团队。

5. 采取奖惩分明和坚定果断的绩效管理方式。确实,这些成功企业的一大共同特点就是重视并培养一种认同感。这些公司把获取认同感作为促使员工突破现有能力水平的一种有效途径。与此同时,他们把容忍平庸的做法视作成功之大敌。

6. 不要流于形式,一味地追求投入度本身。由于目前在技术层面上完全有可能实现精准地记录和追踪员工的工作投入度,一些公司开始采用"公米制管理"。然而,真正成功的雇主更关注成果,而取得成果需要员工为之付出更高的投入。

7. 更加体恤自己的员工。我们对全球成年人开展代表性样本研究,结果显示,只要人们全力投入,工作就完全有可能成为成功人士的生活中心。为了达到此目的,人们开展了广泛辩论,探讨如何让工作变得更有趣、更时髦,甚至更有意义,但不少大公司仍然无法如愿。我们研究的成功范例向我们提示了如何与员工建立感情纽带的秘诀。

做到这些并不容易,但如果你全力以赴实现这了不起的七条秘诀,你也能营建一个人人乐在其中的工作团队。

Ⅳ. Extended Terms and Expressions 词汇拓展训练

Directions: Fill in the following table and try to get familiar with these extended terms and expressions.

Short Form	Full Form and Chinese Translation
GDP	1.
GNP	2.
CPI	3.
PPI	4.
NI	5.
PI	6.
NNP	7.
RPI	8.

Ⅴ. Sentence Translation 句子翻译训练

Directions: Each of the following sentences is followed by two versions of translation. Make a comparison between them and decide which one is better. Then discuss with group members and share your viewpoints.

1. Essentially Xiaomi's profit formula is the opposite of Apple's, which collects its highest profits with the introduction of each model and needs to come up with new model after new model to keep those margins up.

   A. 最为重要的是,"小米"的利润公式是"苹果"的相反面:它获得最大利润是通过介绍每一种型号和需要不断设计新产品来维持最高的利润。

   B. 从本质而言,"小米"的利润公式与"苹果"完全相反:通过推出各类不同型号的产品以及想方设法持续更新产品型号来保持利润增长,从而实现利润最大化。

2. By 2013, China's grain output had continuously increased over ten consecutive years and basically met the food demands of the 1.3 billion Chinese.

   A. 到2013年,中国已实现10年粮食产量连续增长,基本满足了13亿人口的粮食需求。

B. 截至 2013 年，中国的谷物产量已经连续增长超过 10 年，基本达到了 13 亿中国人的食物要求。

3. Researchers found that the act of carefully monitoring the fairness of workplace decisions wears down supervisors both mentally and emotionally.
   A. 研究者发现，为了确保工作中的每一个决策都公平公正，公司主管时刻警惕、小心谨慎，势必令主管精疲力尽，伤透脑筋，苦不堪言。
   B. 研究者发现小心翼翼地监管工作场所中的决定的公正性会在精神方面和情绪方面使公司主管疲惫。

4. I'd like to mention here to you some preferential policies granted by our local government for encouraging foreign investment in the New Economic Development Zone.
   A. 我想在这里告诉你一些由当地政府批准颁布的鼓励新经济开发区外商投资的优惠政策。
   B. 我想借此机会向各位介绍当地政府的一些优惠政策，鼓励外商到新经济开发区投资。

5. 在未来三五年内，微博商业模式将逐渐健全起来，但很难预测此后其潜藏的商机。
   A. The business model for micro-blogging will become fully established over the next three to five years, but it is hard to predict its business potential after that.
   B. During the future three to five years, micro-blogging business model will gradually be improved, but difficult to predict the potential business opportunities behind it.

6. 城乡、区域发展不均衡，内陆某些省份的人均 GDP 仅为沿海地区的三分之一。
   A. The development of urban and rural areas and other regions is unbalanced. The average GDP of inland provinces reached only one third of the coastal regions.
   B. Development is quite uneven between urban and rural areas and among different regions, with the per capita GDP of some inland provinces being just one third of that of the coastal regions.

7. 规则是一种清晰的描述，告诉管理者应该做什么，不应该做什么。
   A. A rule is an explicit statement that tells a manager what he or she ought — or ought not — to do.
   B. A rule is a clear description, telling managers should or shouldn't do what.

8. 控制是一种管理功能，指为了确保组织内各项计划按规定完成而进行的监督和纠偏的过程。

   A. The function of management control lies in the process of overseeing and fault-finding to ensure that all activities are completed according to plan and any mistakes are corrected.

   B. Control is the management function that involves monitoring activities within an organization to ensure that they are being accomplished as planned and correcting any deviations.

Ⅵ. Abstract Translation 摘要翻译训练

Directions: *Go through the list of terminologies and get familiar with these terms. Then try to translate the following abstract into English and learn how to write an abstract in a proper way.*

Terminologies
1. 经济全球化 economic globalization
2. 实证分析 empirical analysis
3. 信息化 informatization
4. 量化研究 quantitative research
5. 单极城市化 monopole urbanization
6. 波动性 variability
7. 经济要素流动 economic factor mobility

经济全球化是否导致了更大的城市
——世界与中国城市的实证分析

摘要：经济全球化与信息化已成为推动世界城市化进程的主要驱动力，但针对经济全球化与城市化之间的量化关系的研究却不多见。通过定量分析，发现经济全球化时代世界大城市发展具有如下主要特点：①大城市规模增长的阶段性特征明显；②大城市增长的重点区域转向亚、非和拉美等新兴工业化国家；③非正规城市区域的扩大成为发展中国家大城市扩张的主导城市形态；④巨型城市的极化效应大于扩散效应，导致典型的二元化城市格局；⑤单极城市化、都市化与网络城市化并存发展。此外，本文从世界和中国两个层面，探讨了经济全球化与大城市增长之间的关系，检验了"全球化导致了更大的城市发展"的观点。同时还分析了经济全球化与大城市增长的波动性关系，结果表明：世界大城市增长的波动性总体上要小于经济要素流动的波动性；而中国经济要素流动的波动性与大城市增长的波动性均较大。

关键词：经济全球化；大城市增长；实证分析

Ⅶ. Academic Debate 学术思辨训练

Directions: *Read the following topic and try to translate the provided viewpoints. Then have a discussion with your group members and find more support for both sides. Hold an English debate in class between two groups. Remember: your arguments can refer to but are not limited to the points provided.*

Debate Topic Compared with the Confucious doctrine advocating loose management and relaxed control, F.W. Taylor's theories of scientific management is a more effective way of management in today's enterprises.

Pros:
1. 儒家宽松的管理模式容易导致员工态度松懈,效率低下。
2. 泰勒大力倡导通过劳动力分工最大限度地提高工作效率。
3. 实践证明,泰勒的管理理论切实有效,得到了广大产业界管理层的认可,并能够大幅提高生产效率。
4. 劳动力分工有助于提高劳动熟练度和判断力,节约劳动转换次数和时间,降低培训费用。
5. 劳动力分工程度越高,个人责任越清楚,工作内容越简单,可以减少劳动监管成本。
6. 劳动力分工有助于技术人员和操作人员增加发明新工具的可能性。

Cons:
1. 泰勒的科学管理方法过于强调流程化、标准化和利润最大化,忽略了人的主观能动性,缺乏人文主义关怀。
2. 高度分工降低了工人对整个生产流程的了解,应变和自动协调能力下降。
3. 高度分工也会导致企业整体应变能力下降,不利于在瞬息万变的市场竞争中取胜。
4. 高度分工容易造成对企业中下层员工不利的分配关系,进而导致劳资关系紧张。
5. 儒家思想中"仁"四最高标准,儒家管理方式提倡"以人为本",缓解了冰冷的机械文明带来的负面影响,为企业管理注入了温情,自然而然也就提高了工作效率。
6. 儒家管理思想提倡"修己安人""克己复礼",管理者必须以自我管理为起点,把员工当做最宝贵的资源进行合理利用。
7. 儒家文化的"中庸之道"提倡适度原则,在"集中"和"放权"之间寻求平衡点,有助于在管理过程中事半功倍。
8. 儒家中庸思想主张"君子之中庸也,君子而时中",即提倡管理者学会"适时而变":任何危机本身都是转机,不抓住机遇等于给别人提供机遇。

Ⅷ. Theoretical Guidance 翻译理论指导

笔译技巧：词性转换

除了英语中的冠词及汉语中的量词和助词，其他词性如名词、动词、形容词、代词、介词、副词、数词、连词等都可以在两大语言体系中实现一一对应。但这并不意味着翻译过程中可以简单地实现词性的"机械对等与转化"。具体来看，英汉词性之间显然呈现异大于同的态势。即使对于相同词性而言，在不同语言中的使用范围、频率、词序等功能也有所不同。总体而言，汉语倾向于用动词，英语倾向于用名词和介词。因此，为了确保译文通顺、自然、流畅，翻译过程中往往需要借助"词性转换"的技巧，例如：汉译英常常用到"动词转名词""动词转介词"，英译汉常常用到"名词转动词""形容词转副词"。

请结合笔译技巧解析视频，完成下列句子翻译，注意巧用词性转换技巧。

英译汉练习：

1. It would not be easy to **talk in general terms** about Western Europe **as** a unit, with its **differences** of climate and culture, its mountains, plains and coasts.

2. They expect us in the European Community to work out policies of aid and trade which will show a **sympathetic understanding** of their own problems.

3. The UN document calls for the **settlement** of the Middle East conflicts on the basis of Israeli **withdrawal** from occupied territories and Arab **acknowledgement** of Israel's right to exist.

4. ... and that government **of** the people, **by** the people, **for** the people, shall not perish from the earth.

汉译英练习：

1. 到了徐州见着父亲，**看见**满院狼藉的东西，又**想起**祖母，我不禁簌簌地留下眼泪。

2. 我们这些小国终将发现，资本主义就其本性而言，就是**帝国主义**，就是**剥削**，因此我们会变成欧美资本主义国家的卫星国。

3. 贸易量**大幅提升**，给两国**带来**了益处。

4. 她身穿一件深红外衣，袖子卷起，露出**雪白的**手臂。

Chapter 2　Language & Culture

语 言 文 化

Ⅰ. Academic Background 学术背景汇报

Directions: *Study the following questions before class and try to search for some relevant information. Then discuss these questions with your group members. Give a brief introduction to the discipline of linguistics and present it in class.*

1. How do you define the discipline of linguistics?
2. Why do we need linguistic studies?
3. Applied linguistics is an interdisciplinary field. How do we benefit from applied linguistics?
4. What is culture? What is the correlation between language and culture?

Ⅱ. E-C Academic Translation 英汉学术翻译

Directions: *Study the notes in advance. Then read the following passage carefully and translate it into Chinese with the help of the notes supplied. Try to enrich your academic vocabulary and sentence patterns.*

1. vanish　v. 销声匿迹；(突然)消失
2. linguist　n. 语言学家
   linguistic adj. 语言(学)的
   linguistics n. 语言学
3. field work　田野调查；实地考察
4. stir　n. 轰动　v. 搅拌；激发
5. mourn　v. 悼念；悲伤
6. extraordinary　adj. 意想不到的；非凡的
7. die out　灭绝；逐渐消失
8. staggering　adj. 令人难以相信的；惊人的
9. in danger of　处于……危险之中
10. assimilation　n. 吸收；同化
    assimilate　v. (使)同化；吸收；透彻理解；使接受
11. genocide　n. 种族灭绝；大屠杀
12. displace　v. 离开家园
13. trauma　n. 外伤；精神创伤；痛苦经历
14. stay put　留在原地；保持原样
15. dominant　adj. 首要的；占支配地位的；显著的

16. bilingualism   n. 双语现象
17. give way to   让位于……；给……让路
18. monolingualism   n. 单语现象
19. diversity   n. 多样性；多元化
20. in the case of   就……而言
21. intellectual   adj. 智力的；脑力的
22. encapsulate   v. 封装；压缩；概括

Vanishing Voices

In 1995, linguist Bruce Connell was doing some field work in Cameroon. He found a language called Kasabe, which no Westerner had studied before. It had just one speaker left, a man called Bogon. Connell had no time on that visit, so he decided to return to Cameroon a year later. He arrived in the early winter, only to learn that Bogon had died on November 5th.

On November 4th, Kasabe existed as one of the world's languages; on November 6th, it did not. The event might have caused a stir in Bogon's village. If you are the last speaker of a language, you are often considered special in your community. But outside the village, who knew or mourned the passing of what he stood for?

There is nothing unusual about Bogon's story. Communities have come and gone throughout history, taking their languages with them. But, judging by the standards of the past, what is happening today is extraordinary. There are now about 6,000 languages in the world. Of these, about half are going to die out during the next century.

The full statistics are frightening. There are 51 languages with only one speaker left — 28 in Australia alone. There are more than 3,000 with fewer than 10,000 speakers; and a staggering 5,000 languages with fewer than 100,000 speakers. Ninety-six per cent of the world's languages are spoken by only 4% of its people. No wonder so many are in danger of dying.

Many things can kill a language, from natural disasters to cultural assimilation and genocide. On July 17th, 1998, an earthquake in Papua New Guinea killed more than 2,200 people and displaced a further 10,000, and several villages were completely destroyed. As the survivors have moved away, will these communities and thus their languages survive the trauma of displacement?

Even if a people stays put, their language may still die as a result of cultural assimilation. At first, there is pressure on the people to speak the dominant language. Then there is a period of bilingualism. Finally, bilingualism starts to decline, with the old language giving way to the new. This leads to the third stage, in which the younger generation finds its old language less and less relevant. This is often accompanied by a feeling of shame about using the old language, which gradually leads to monolingualism.

Is language death such a disaster? As long as a few hundred or even a couple of thousand languages survive, you might say, that is sufficient. It is not. We should care about dying languages for the same reason that we care when a species of animal or plant dies. It reduces the diversity of our planet. In the case of language, we are talking about intellectual and cultural diversity, not biological diversity, but the issues are the same.

Many different skills and characteristics enable a species to survive in different environments, and the need to maintain linguistic diversity stands on the shoulders of this argument. Encapsulated within a language is most of a community's history, a large part of its cultural identity and a wealth of knowledge which the rest of the world can access.

Ⅲ. C-E Academic Translation 汉英学术翻译

Directions: *Study the notes in advance, and then read the following passage carefully and translate it into English with the help of the notes supplied. Try to enrich your academic vocabulary and sentence patterns.*

1. 舶来语 loanword; borrowed word
2. 通用语 lingua franca; a common language
3. 演变 evolve
4. 大杂烩 a mixture of
5. 入侵 invade; invasion
6. 外族入侵者 foreign invader
7. 征服 conquest; conquer
8. 吸收 uptake; absorb; assimilate; adopt
9. 多样性的 diverse
   多样性 diversity
10. 融合体 a blended version of; a combination of
11. 有影响力的 influential
12. 核心词 core word
13. 北欧移民 Scandinavian settler
14. 统治阶级 ruling class
15. 文艺复兴时期 the Renaissance
16. 特别努力 make a deliberate/special effort
17. 顺理成章地 be natural to do ...; as a matter of course
18. 远航探索 voyage exploration
19. 殖民扩张 colonial expansion
20. 殖民统治;殖民主义 colonialism
21. 经久不衰 the continued prevalence; everlasting; enduring
22. 崛起 the rise of; rise abruptly

舶 来 语

英语为现代世界的"通用语",是科学研究、国际商务及互通交流的通用语言。通过与其他文化体系相互交融并经历漫长岁月的洗礼,英语逐步演变成了一种融合众多语言的大杂烩。语言学家认为，外族入侵者屡次征服英国致使英语经历了一次又一次的舶来高潮。英语吸收了各种不同语言的词汇，这些词汇通常被称为"舶来语"。英语也因此成为全世界最丰富多彩的语言之一。

　　从公元450年左右到11世纪，英格兰屡次遭遇外来者的入侵，这些侵略者将他们的语言带到了这里。随着每一次入侵，不列颠民族适时调整自己的语言，将外族语和本族语相融合，创造出了一种多语言融合体。其中，对英语影响最深的语言包括：公元700年入侵者带来的西日耳曼语；8至9世纪北欧入侵者带来的古挪威语；以及最重要的，1066年诺曼征服时期所带来的法语和拉丁语。

　　正如其他语言，英语也使用核心词指称我们熟悉的日常事物。这些核心词大都起源于日耳曼语，属于北欧移民带来的一部分英语词汇。许多核心词在此后几个世纪里并没有太大的变化，能相当容易地辨认出来。诺曼入侵者给英语留下了许多法语词汇，主要涉及战争、政府、法律、艺术和时尚等方面。这些领域对于一个强大的统治阶级而言至关重要。16世纪文艺复兴时期，学习研究蔚然成风。很多人热衷于学习拉丁语和希腊语，以及古代文化。当时，人们特别热衷于丰富英语词汇，使之满足一系列艺术和学术的需要。当然这样一来，人们似乎是顺理成章地借用来自拉丁语和希腊语的新词。随后的几个世纪里，随着全球探险和殖民扩张，远航者带回来新的产品和新的体验，以及这些产品和体验所对应的新的词汇。例如在殖民统治时期，随着英国与亚洲地区交流的日益频繁，英语中融入了许多亚洲词汇，比如jungle(丛林)和yoga(瑜伽)。

　　舶来语经久不衰，这表明在全球化背景下，不同文化之间的交流日益紧密。全球化网络媒体的崛起，以及国际交流的日益加深，使得人们对通用语言的需求不断上升。

Ⅳ. Extended Terms and Expressions 词汇拓展训练

Directions: *Fill in the following chart and try to get familiar with these extended terms and expressions.*

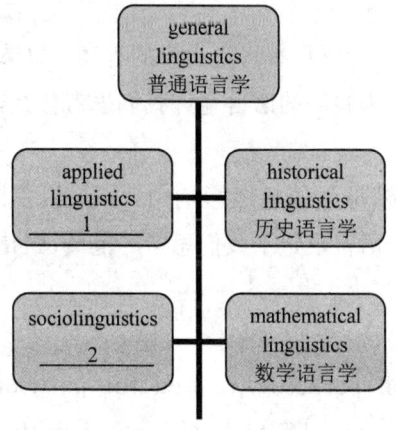

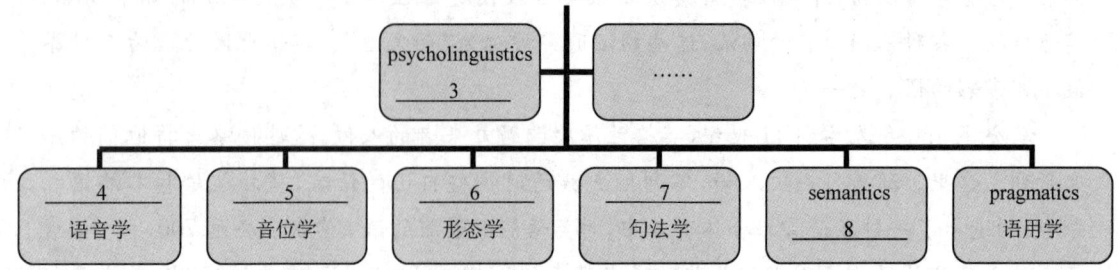

Ⅴ. Sentence Translation 句子翻译训练

Directions: *Each of the following sentences is followed by two versions of translation. Make a comparison between them and decide which one is better. Then discuss with group members and share your viewpoints.*

1. Language acquisition is studied by linguists, psychologists and applied linguists to enable them to understand the processes used in learning a language, to help identify stages in the developmental process, and to give a better understanding of the nature of language.

    A. 语言习得被语言学家、心理学家和应用语言学家研究，目的是为了使他们了解学习一门语言的过程，帮助他们确定发展阶段，并对语言的自然属性作出更好的理解。

    B. 语言学家、心理学家和应用语言学家研究语言习得以便了解语言学习所经历的阶段，帮助他们明确语言发展过程的各个阶段，并更好地理解语言的本质。

2. This maxim offers us the key to unlocking the real force of the mother tongue: if different languages influence our minds in different ways, this is not because of what our language allows us to think but rather because of what it habitually obliges us to think about.

    A. 这一格言向我们提供了母语具有真正力量的答案：如果不同语言以不同的方式影响我们的思维，那不是因为我们的语言允许我们思考什么，而是因为它习惯性地迫使我们思考什么。

    B. 这一箴言帮助我们解锁母语的超级影响力：如果说不同语言造就了不同的思维方式，那么这并不是由于语言限定了我们思考的范畴，而是由于语言促使我们习惯性地遵循特定的思维模式。

3. ESP (English for special purposes) is used for particular and restricted types of communication (e.g. for medical reports, scientific writing, air-traffic control) which

contains lexical, grammatical, and other linguistic features which are different from ordinary language.

A. ESP(特殊目的英语)被运用于特定的、限制性的交际(如用于医疗报告、科技文献或航空管理),包含与普通语言不同的词汇、语法和其他语言特征。

B. ESP(专门用途英语)用于特定的、有限用途的交际(如用于医学报告、科技文章或空中交通调度)。这类语言在词汇、语法和其他语言特征上有别于普通语言。

4. For half a century an influential group of Western linguists, led by Chomsky, have argued that human knowledge develops from structures, processes, and "ideas" which are in the mind at birth (i.e. are innate), rather than from the environment, and that these are responsible for the basic structure of language and how it is learned.

A. 半个世纪以来,以乔姆斯基为首的一派具有影响力的西方语言学家认为,人类的知识来自头脑中与生俱来的(即天生的)结构、过程和"理念",而不是来自环境。这些先天因素是语言基本结构的基础,也是人类语言习得的基础。

B. 长达半个世纪之久,乔姆斯基领导一批具有影响力的西方语言学家。他们争论人类的知识来自结构、过程和"理念",这些是头脑中生来就有的(即天生的)的东西,而不是来自环境。正是这些东西负责语言的基本结构并决定语言是如何被人们学习的。

5. 最近,科学家对44名懂西班牙语和英语的双语老年人进行了调查,通过比较个体使用每一种语言的熟练程度衡量他们的语言能力。调查发现,双语能力越强,对阿尔茨海默病的抵抗力也越强;高水平的双语能力亦有助于推迟发病年龄。

A. In a recent study of 44 elderly Spanish-English bilinguals, scientists found that individuals with a higher degree of bilingualism — measured through a comparative evaluation of proficiency in each language — were more resistant than others to the onset of Alzheimer's disease: the higher the degree of bilingualism, the later the age of onset.

B. Scientists recently do an investigation about 44 old people able to speak Spanish and English and evaluate their language ability by comparing their language proficiency. The investigation finds that the stronger the bi-language ability, the stronger they are to resist Alzheimer; high level of bi-language can put off the age of disease.

6. 一种语言之所以成为主导语言，是因为它在该国中有较高的声望或地位，为政府所青睐，并拥有最多的使用者。

    A. A kind of language becomes a major language because it has a higher reputation or position in the country, is liked by the government, and has the largest population using the language.

    B. A language may become the dominant language because it has more prestige or higher status in the country, is favored by the government, and has the largest number of speakers.

7. 在第二语言或外语学习中，为了有效习得语言，有必要让学习者理解所输入的语言，其中包括略高于其现有语言能力的语言项目。

    A. In learning a second language or a foreign language, in order to get a language effectively, learners need to understand the input language including linguistic units which are a little higher than the learners' present language ability.

    B. In second or foreign language learning, for language acquisition to occur, it is necessary for learners to understand the input language which contains linguistic items that are slightly beyond the learners' present linguistic competence.

8. 语码转换可以发生在对话过程中，一方使用一种语言，另一方却用别的语言来回答；一个人可能开始时讲某种语言，中途却换成另一种语言，有时甚至一个句子只说了一半就改变语种。

    A. Code-switching can take place in a conversation when one speaker uses one language and the other answers in a different language. A person may start speaking one language and then change to another one in the middle of the speech, or sometimes even in the middle of a sentence.

    B. Code-switching can occur in the process of a dialogue. One party uses a kind of language, but the other party answers in another language; a man may speak one language at the beginning, but change to another language in the middle, sometimes the language is changed even a sentence has not been finished.

Ⅵ. Abstract Translation 摘要翻译训练

Directions: *Go through the list of terminologies and get familiar with these terms. Then try to translate the following abstract into English and learn how to write an abstract in a proper way.*

Terminologies
1. 认知语言学 cognitive linguistics
2. 系统功能语言学 systemic functional linguistics
3. 元功能 metafunction *n.*
4. [语]语义学 semantics *n.*
5. 意义潜势 meaning potential
6. 符号学 semiotics *n.*

系统功能语言学的认知观

摘要：本文讨论20世纪80年代认知语言学研究兴起后，系统功能语言学家对认知、认知科学和认知语言学的观点。主要整理汇报韩礼德散见在不同时期有关认知的评述和观点，间或谈到其他系统功能语言学家的观点和工作。具体内容包括认知在系统功能语言学框架中的地位，如心理过程、三大元功能、语义层和意义潜势等。在此基础上，讨论认知与语言、语义、语法、语言习得、符号学以及与认知功能框架的关系。最后，作者认为系统功能语言学和认知语言学在探索认知与意义的道路上是同路人的关系。

关键词：认知；意义；认知语言学；系统功能语言学

Ⅶ. Academic Debate 学术思辨训练

Directions: *Read the following topic and try to translate the provided viewpoints. Then have a discussion with your group members and find more support for both sides. Hold an English debate in class between two groups. Remember：your arguments can refer to but are not limited to the points provided.*

Debate Topic   Nowadays, with advanced translation software, it is not necessary for Chinese students to learn a foreign language any more.

Pros：
1. 翻译软件十分发达，无论是书面语还是口语，都可以瞬间完成双语转换。
2. 学习外语主要为了方便语言不通的双方开展交流，现代技术解决了这一难题，因此没有必要花时间学习外语。
3. 目前，从幼儿园到大学，每个人都在学习外语，并投入大量的人力、物力和财力，"外语学习热"造成社会资源的巨大浪费，中国学生还不如多学一点"数理化"和"计算机"。
4. 中国综合国力日益强大，世界各地越来越多的人开始学习汉语，这也从另一个侧面表明中国学生没有必要学习外语了。

Cons：
1. 不可否认，翻译软件的确日益发达，能够实现双语实时转换，但是翻译质量仍有待提高，外交、商贸、科技等重大交际场合不宜直接使用翻译软件，以免造成重大损失。
2. 提高外语阅读能力，有助于更加便捷地查阅外文书籍和文献资料，增长见识，而一味依靠翻译软件容易产生误解。
3. 学好外语，出国深造，可以不断提升自己。出国留学不可能无时无刻都依赖翻译软件，这不但不方便，而且国外高校也不允许，因此他们会对入学者的外语能力提出要求。
4. 精通一国或多国外语可以拓宽自己的就业面，极大提升核心竞争力。
5. 掌握一口流利的外语，能够直接和外国人沟通，增进双方的理解和友谊，也能够在交流过程中积极传播中国文化，营造风趣幽默的氛围，这些都是翻译软件不可比拟的。
6. 语言和思维、文化紧密相连，学习外语也是开发智力、丰富思维方式、提高跨文化交际能力的一种很好的训练方法。

Ⅷ. Theoretical Guidance 翻译理论指导

笔译技巧：增词减词

"增词"与"减词"看似属于相互矛盾、相互对立的思维过程，实则是翻译中十分常见而又有效的补偿手段，都是为了实现灵活对等，忠实、通顺地再现原作的意义与风格。"增词"是指为了补足语际转换造成的语义缺失和保持译文结构完整，通过解释原作文化背景以及补充译文修辞手段等方式，对译文作适当补充，其原则是"不额外增添意义"；"减词"是指完整保留原义的前提下，删除目标语中显得累赘、啰嗦，甚至可有可无的词语，例如只具备语法功能的一些虚词，其原则是"不破坏或删改原意"。

请结合笔译技巧解析视频,完成下列句子翻译,注意巧用增词减词技巧。

英译汉练习:

1. **Nations** have utilized different economic resources; **people** have developed different skills.

2. Part-time waitress applicants who have worked at a job would receive preference **over those who haven't**.

3. At this sight, the blond boy immediately **crossed himself**.

4. The Shanghai **law** looked into this matter immediately.

汉译英练习:

1. 这款新推出的饮料可谓**男女老少皆宜**。

2. 这座宝塔的屋顶是用**浓淡不同的**黄色和绿色琉璃瓦盖成的。

3. 我们希望把下一代培养成**忠于祖国**、**尽职尽责**的中国人。

4. 勇敢**过度**,即成蛮勇;疼爱**过度**,即成溺爱;节俭**过度**,即成贪婪。

Chapter 3 Sociological Studies

社 会 研 究

Ⅰ. Academic Background 学术背景汇报

Directions: Study the following questions before class and try to search for some relevant information. Then discuss these questions with your group members. Give a brief introduction to the discipline of sociology and present it in class.

1. What does the discipline of sociology mainly cover?
2. What are the main theories of sociology?
3. Why do we carry out sociological studies?
4. Can you mention some practical applications of sociology in our daily life?

Ⅱ. E-C Academic Translation 英汉学术翻译

Directions: Study the notes in advance. Then read the following passage carefully and translate it into Chinese with the help of the notes supplied. Try to enrich your academic vocabulary and sentence patterns.

1. pandemic *n.* (全国或全球性)流行病 *adj.* (疾病)大流行的;普遍的
2. rage *n.* 狂怒;暴怒 *v.* 发怒;激烈进行
3. vaccine *n.* 疫苗
4. nationalism *n.* 民族主义
5. energize *vt.* 使充满热情;给(某人)增添能量、精力或干劲
6. play up one's strength 发挥自身优势
7. supply chain 供应链
8. humanitarian aids 人道主义援助
9. first nature 第一属性
10. uphold *v.* 支持;维持
11. stride towards 迈向
12. be bound to 一定要;决心;注定
13. inject *v.* 注射(药物等);增加(品质)
14. impetus *n.* 动力;推动;促进;刺激
15. resurgence *n.* 复苏;复兴
16. unswervingly *adv.* 坚定不移地;矢志不渝地;毫不动摇地
17. hold up 举起;支撑
18. a community with a shared future for humanity 人类命运共同体
19. the principles of extensive consultation, joint contribution and shared benefits 共商共建共享原则
20. multilateralism *n.* 多边主义

21. *Charter of the United Nations*《联合国宪章》
22. persistently *adv.* 固执地；坚持地；坚持不懈地
23. narrow down   变窄；缩减

Pandemic

Currently, the COVID-19 pandemic is still raging globally and the world economy still faces the risk of declining. Vaccines become the key to fighting against the pandemic. China opposes the so-called "vaccine nationalism" and insists that we should make vaccine a global public good. So far, we have offered anti-pandemic supplies to more than 160 countries and international organizations worldwide and are providing the urgently needed vaccines to over 100 countries and international organizations in different ways, greatly energizing the global pandemic prevention and control efforts. China will continue to play up its strength to maintain the supply chain stability of anti-pandemic supplies. We will also actively keep offering humanitarian aids to countries in need. And China will uphold the "first nature" of vaccines as a public good, striving to make safe and reliable vaccines accessible and affordable to more developing countries.

At the same time, we will uphold opening-up and cooperation, and jointly promote the world economic recovery with other countries. We have successfully started the 14th Five-Year Plan, speeding up in building a new system of the open economy at a higher level. A China which is striding towards quality development in all aspects will bring new development opportunities for all countries; while a China keeping opening-up is bound to inject more impetus to the global economic resurgence.

Humanity should be united as a whole. Life and health, existence and development should be the rights equally accessible to people all around the world. China will unswervingly hold up the banner of building a community with a shared future for humanity, insist on the principles of extensive consultation, joint contribution and shared benefits, practice true multilateralism, safeguard the international order based on the *Charter of the United Nations*, persistently improve global governance, so as to establish a community of health for humankind. China will also maintain the world peace and stability with other countries and narrow down the development gap, creating a better future together with the international community.

Ⅲ. C-E Academic Translation 汉英学术翻译

Directions: *Study the notes in advance. Then read the following passage carefully and translate it into English with the help of the notes supplied. Try to enrich your academic vocabulary and sentence patterns.*

1. 人口普查 population census
2. 开启；着手 embark on
3. 全面 in all respects; thoroughly; comprehensively
4. 内在需求 inherent need
5. 转变；转化 transformation; transition; shift
6. 完善；优化 optimize; improve; optimization; improvement
7. 增长动力 growth impetus
8. 攻关期；关键期 critical period
9. 发展方式；发展模式 growth pattern; development mode
10. 查清，摸清 figure out; identify; have/acquire a (full/better) understanding of ...
11. 国情 national situations/conditions
12. 结构 composition; structure; distribution
13. 迫切需要 an urgent need for; be urgently needed for
14. 人口发展 demographic growth; growth of population
15. 显著的 prominent; significant
16. 劳动年龄人口 working-age population
17. 波动下降 fluctuating decrease
18. 流动人口 migrant/floating population
19. 提供基础 serve as the basis; set up the basis
20. 基础设施 infrastructure
21. 布局 layout
22. 服务网点 service networks

人口普查

作为全球人口第一大国、世界第二大经济体，中国十年一度的人口普查是一次重大国情国力调查，将呈现中国人口在数量、结构、分布等方面的最新情况。2020年11月中国开始了第七次人口普查。人口普查将为开启全面建设社会主义现代化国家新征程提供科学准确的统计信息支持。

人口普查是推动经济高质量发展的内在需求。当前，我国经济正处于转变发展方式、优化经济结构、转换增长动力的攻关期。及时查清人口数量、结构和分布这一基本国情，摸清人力资源结构信息，才能够更加准确地把握需求结构、城乡结构、区域结构、产业结构等状况，为推动经济高质量发展，建设现代化经济体系提供有力的支持。

人口普查是完善人口发展战略和政策体系，促进人口长期均衡发展的迫切需要。自2010年第六次全国人口普查以来，我国人口发展的内在动力和外部条件发生了显著改变。人口总规模增长减缓，劳动年龄人口波动下降，老龄化程度不断加深。全面查清我国人口数量、结构、分布、城乡住房等方面的最新情况有助于了解人口增长、劳动力供给、流动人口变化情况,摸清老年人口规模,为制定和完善未来收入、消费、教育、就业、养老、医疗、社会保障等政策措施提供基础,也为教育和医疗机构布局、儿童和老人服务基础设施建设、工商业服务网点分布、城乡道路建设等提供依据。

Ⅳ. Extended Terms and Expressions 词汇拓展训练

Directions: *Fill in the following chart and try to get familiar with these extended terms and expressions.*

Definitions	Disciplines
1. science of society, social institutions and social relationships, especially the systematic study of the development, structure, interaction and collective behavior of organized groups of human beings	1. _____
2. a border field which denotes the analysis of the inter-relationship between social structures and political institutions, and between the society and the state	2. _____
3. study of educational objectives and organization in the light of an analysis of the group life as a whole	3. _____
4. a branch of sociology concerned with study of the origins, stages and laws of social life and social institutions	4. _____
5. the sociological study of the historical processes involved in cultural phenomena (such as art, philosophy and religion)	5. _____
6. a branch of sociology dealing with the study of rural communities and the rural way of life	6. _____
7. a branch of sociology dealing with the development of urban communities and their effect upon society	7. _____
8. sociological analysis directed at institutions and social relationships within and largely controlled or affected by industry	8. _____

Ⅴ. Sentence Translation 句子翻译训练

Directions: *Each of the following sentences is followed by two versions of translation. Make a comparison between them and decide which one is better. Then discuss with group members and share your viewpoints.*

1. American presidents tend to be judged less by the good deeds they set in motion than by how well they respond to crises.
   A. 美国人评价总统，一般先看他是否能临危不乱，力挽狂澜，治国之道还在其次。
   B. 比起启动有效的措施，美国总统更倾向于通过应对危机的能力被世人评判。

2. You don't have to become a social butterfly, flitting from one event to another, but it's important to have connections and contacts.
   A. 你没有必要成为交际花，闪现于各种社交场所，但是保持联系和接触是非常重要的。
   B. 这并不是要求你成为一个交际高手，出入于各种交际场所，但是与外界保持联系和接触这一点非常重要的。

3. Children who are emotionally abused and neglected face similar and sometimes worse mental health problems as children who are physically or sexually abused, yet psychological abuse is rarely addressed in prevention programs or in treating victims.
   A. 与遭受体罚或性虐待的孩子相比，在情感方面遭受虐待与冷遇的孩子面临着相同甚至更为严重的精神健康问题，然而预防方案或受害治疗方案往往很少涉及如何解决心理虐待问题。
   B. 遭受情感虐待与情感忽视的孩子与遭受身体虐待或者性虐待的孩子面临着相同——有时则是更为严重的精神健康问题，尽管预防方案或治疗受害者很少解决心理虐待。

4. Freedom is the basic right of a human being, who is supposed to do whatever he or she wants; but certain customs of the family or society, or sometimes the responsibilities or the pressure of career etc. do not let him or her fulfill it.
   A. 自由是一个人的基本权利，他或她应该做任何想要做的事情，但家庭或社会的某些传统，或有时候是一种责任感或事业带来的压力让他或她不能做自己想做的事。
   B. 自由是人类的基本权利，每个人应该做任何自己想要做的事情，但家庭或社会的某些习俗，亦或是来自事业的责任和压力等种种原因让人们不能做自己想做的事。

5. 新冠肺炎疫情对许多全球最大经济体的巨大冲击，可能没有几个月前经济学家担心的那么严重。
   A. The big shock to many of the global biggest economies from the corona virus pandemic may not be as big as economists feared just a few months ago.
   B. The corona virus pandemic has brought about a huge shock to many world's largest economies, which seems less serious than what the economists worried in the prerious.

6. 任何以牺牲安全为代价的核能发展都难以持续,都不能带来真正的发展。
   A. Any development at the cost of nuclear energy safety cannot last long, which would not bring any real development.
   B. Developing nuclear energy at the expense of security can neither be sustainable nor bring real development.

7. 自中国实行改革开放政策以来,持续 30 多年的努力使中国人民的生活水平在一代人之内得到大幅提升。
   A. Thanks to the persistent endeavor over 30 years since the adoption of the Reform and Opening-up Policy, the living standards of the Chinese people has been substantially improved within a generation.
   B. Since China adopted the Reform and Opening-up Policy, more than 30 years' efforts have made Chinese people's lives greatly improved between a generation of people.

8. 我们可以把社会学描述为研究社会结构和社会制度的科学。社会学的研究内容通常划分为现代社会的阶级结构、家庭、犯罪和反常、宗教等类别。
   A. We can describe sociology as a science of researching social structures and systems, and social research content can usually be divided into class structure of modern societies, family, crime and abmormality, religion, etc.
   B. Sociology could be described as the study of social structures and social institutions, and sociological work is often divided into such catogaries as the class structure of modern societies, family, crime and deviance, religion, and so on.

Ⅵ. Abstract Translation 摘要翻译训练

Directions: *Go through the list of terminologies and get familiar with these terms. Then try to trunslate the following abstract into English and learn how to write an abstract in a proper way.*

Terminologies
1. 城镇化 urbanization
2. 产业化 industrialization
3. 推进模式;发展模式 development mode/pattern
4. 动力机制;驱动程序 driver
5. 空间模式 spatial pattern

6. 整体推动；全面发展 all-round development
7. 跳跃性；不连续性 discontinuity
8. 自发的 spontaneous
9. 民间社会 civil society
10. 中央商务区 central business district
11. 良性的 benign

中国城镇化"推进模式"研究

摘要：从城镇化的动力机制和空间模式两个视角理解中国城镇化"推进模式"的特征，发现中国城镇化的突出特征是政府主导、大范围规划、整体推动、土地的国家或集体所有、空间上有明显的跳跃性、民间社会尚不具备自发推进城镇化的条件等。可将我国城镇化"推进模式"区分为七种类型；建立开发区、建设新区和新城、城市扩建、旧城改造、建设中央商务区、乡镇产业化和村庄产业化。政府主导的城镇化推进模式充分体现了中国的制度创新性及灵活性，但如何更尊重客观经济规律，促进政府与民众良性互动，以实现城市增长的公平主义，亦为亟待研究和解决的重大问题。

关键词：城镇化；推进模式；空间模式

Ⅶ. Academic Debate 学术思辨训练

Directions: *Read the following topic and try to translate the provided viewpoints. Then have a discussion with your group members and find more support for both sides. Hold an English debate in class between two groups. Remember：your arguments can refer to but are not limited to the points provided.*

Debate Topic Working experience is more important than schooling and academic certificate.

Pros：
1. 学历只代表一个人曾经在哪个学校学习了什么专业、学习了多长年限等。学习经历，只是一个完成阶段性学习的凭证，具有很大的局限性。
2. 俗话说："纸上得来终觉浅，绝知此事要躬行。"在校期间习得的知识总体而言仍然停留在理论的层面上，知识不等于能力，学习时长不代表优秀。

3. 学历是静态的、有限的,而经历是无限的,代表着与时俱进、不断磨砺。知识的获取只能通过生活和工作中的各种经历来沉淀。
4. 一个人的综合素质很难直接通过学历体现出来,丰富的工作经历和社会经历才是个人价值的体现。
5. 人无完人,只有经历过,才能知道自己的不足,从而不断完善自我。
6. 只有投身社会,才能拥有必要的交际能力,建立更广的人脉关系,人生道路才能越走越宽。这也是学历无法取代的。

Cons:

1. 能力很难量化,学历是能力量化的一个公认的准绳和工具。学历可以用来证明一个人的毅力、目标、胸襟、判断力、记忆力、逻辑性和执行力,这些都是能力的具体表现。
2. 学习是一个很难、很累的过程,需要长期的科学规划和脚踏实地的付出。一个人如果无法在学业上取得佳绩,那么也就证明其能力不足,大多数情况下很难得到社会的认可。
3. 学历是敲门砖,有较高的学历,起码我们就拥有参与高水平竞争的机会;反之,你很可能连展示自己能力的机会都没有。
4. 虽然有言道:"三百六十行,行行出状元",但是自古以来人们还是默认一个法则——"万般皆下品,惟有读书高"。
5. 不可否认,有时候由于家庭、经济、疾病等阻力的困扰,一些真正有能力的人失去了学习的机会。有能力但没有学历,需要付出成倍的努力才能得到社会的认可。
6. 人们常常拿"高学历、低能力"来说事儿,却很少说"低学历、低能力",这恰恰说明了学历和能力之间存在某种正相关,因此"学历较低能力也较低"就不足为奇、避而不谈了。

Ⅷ. Theoretical Guidance 翻译理论指导

笔译技巧:分译合译

英语作为"形合"语言,基于发达的从句、分词、不定式等语法结构,倾向于使用长句,尤其是在书面语中更是如此。而中文为"意合"语言,行文多用短句,通过断句和语序等手段表达语义。在翻译的过程中,为了行文流畅、达意清晰,有时需要将结构复杂、信息量大的长句拆分为多个词组、从句或者独立的句子,这种技巧即分译。同理,为了言简意赅,避免罗唆和重复,有时需要将句子的几个部分甚至是几个句子进行合并,这种技巧即合译。总之,"分译"与"合译"的目的都是为了使译文符合译入语的语序表达习惯,强调功能对等,完整再现原文。

> 请结合笔译技巧解析视频,完成下列句子翻译,注意巧用分译合译技巧。

英译汉练习:

1. But this naval competition **strained** the Liberal Government's **principles** as well as their **budgets**.

2. Law enforcement cannot **responsibly** stand aloof.

3. **It is a truth universally acknowledged** that a single man in possession of a good fortune must be in want of a wife.

4. The era of blatant discrimination ended in the **1960s through** the courageous actions of thousands of blacks **participating** in peaceful marches and sit-ins **to force** Southern states to implement the Federal desegregation laws in schools and public accommodation.

汉译英练习:

1. 做你喜欢做的事,<u>又</u>得到认可,<u>那</u>才叫棒。

2. 至于外商独资企业,外方提供所有资金,<u>赚取</u>所有<u>利润</u>,同时<u>承担</u>所有<u>风险</u>。

3. <u>由于人民生活水平不断提高以及采取计划生育政策</u>,中国的家庭结构发生着缓慢的<u>实质性变化</u>。必须根据<u>这一历史背景</u>考虑如何解决人口老龄化问题。

4. 年青人**在校求学**,**各得其所**,**目标明确**,受到同伴们的照顾和尊重。而当他们一踏出校门,**却**找不到自己孜孜以求的第一份工作,**不得不**面对有生以来的第一次失业。**面对这种情况**,无论是家庭还是学校都没有帮助他们做好准备。

_____

Chapter 4　Law & Regulation

法 律 法 规

Ⅰ. Academic Background 学术背景汇报

irections: *Study the following questions before class and try to search for some relevant information. Then discuss these questions with your group members. Give a brief introduction to the discipline of law and present it in class.*

1. Why do we need laws and regulations in the society?
2. How many sub-disciplines are there concerning law?
3. What do you think of "the rule of law"?
4. In your opinion, what is the co-relation between democracy and nomocracy?

Ⅱ. E-C Academic Translation 英汉学术翻译

irections: *Study the notes in advance. Then read the following passage carefully and translate it into Chinese with the help of the notes supplied. Try to enrich your academic vocabulary and sentence patterns.*

1. pioneer　*n.* 先锋；先驱
2. generate　*v.* 产生；生成
3. revenue　*n.* 收益；营业额
4. shingle　*n.* （诊所或律师事务所挂的）招牌
5. a single shingle　小公司
6. headcount　*n.* 员工人数
7. corporate　*adj.* 公司的；法人的
8. partnership　*n.* 合作关系；合伙企业
9. rehearse　*v.* 排练；排演；重复
10. violate　*v.* 违反
11. assembly　*n.* 集会；议会；装配
12. line up　排成一列
13. a chunk of　大量的
14. upgrade　*v.* 提升；提高；改进
15. take advantage of scale　利用规模效益
16. indignant　*adj.* 愤慨的；愤愤不平的
17. regulate　*v.* 管理；调节
18. delegate　*v.* 授权；委托
19. model rules　范式规定；示范性规则
20. the reality on the ground　（不争的）现实
21. baron　*n.* 工商业巨头
22. serf　*n.* （旧时的）农奴；效力者
23. boost　*vt.* 使增长；促进；增加

Operational Mode of American Law Firms

Jacoby & Myers was a pioneer in fighting for lawyers' right to advertise. Today, the firm is trying to win another suit to change the rules of America's legal industry, which generated revenues of $261 billion in the 12 months to September. If successful, the suit would allow non-lawyer investors to put money in a law firm — first in New York, New Jersey and Connecticut, which Jacoby & Myers has picked as a target, and then probably elsewhere. Currently, law firms, whether a "single shingle" or one like Jones Day (the biggest American firm by headcount with more than 2,400 lawyers and 800 partners), may have only one corporate form anywhere except the District of Columbia: a partnership owned only by lawyers.

The arguments in the case are well-rehearsed — and self-interested. Jacoby & Myers says that the existing rules violate its freedoms of speech and assembly. It has lined up non-lawyer investors who would buy a chunk of the firm and share its profits, if allowed to do so. Andrew Finkelstein, the firm's managing partner, says that outside capital would allow the firm to upgrade technology and take advantage of scale. His aim is simply to give more clients with low incomes access to justice, and he says with the tone of a man indignant that anyone could oppose such a thing.

Equally predictably, the American Bar Association (ABA), which indirectly sets the rules that regulate lawyers (states delegate these to their courts, which usually follow the ABA's "model rules"), opposes the change. Lawyers, it argues, are not business people with a duty to the bottom line, but professionals with an ethical duty to their clients' best interests. Outside investors could push lawyers to file junk suits or take quick settlements to maximize profits.

Yet the reality on the ground in America suggests that change is badly needed. Many law firms are less than the sum of their parts. Partners are semi-independent barons, complete with associate lawyers as serfs. Nearly all work is billed by the hour, meaning efficiency destroys revenue. By contrast, an integrated firm with professional managers and modern computer systems could develop processes that are repeatable. A few small American firms are already trying to run themselves more like modern businesses, and are delighting clients with quick, high-quality work and predictable fees. Allowing outside investment would boost the number and size of such firms.

III. C-E Academic Translation 汉英学术翻译

Directions: *Study the notes in advance. Then read the following passage carefully and* translate it into English with the help of the notes supplied. Try to enrich your academic vocabulary and sentence patterns.

1. 粤港澳大湾区 the Guangdong-Hong Kong-Macao Greater Bay Area
2. 部署 deploy
3. 最高人民检察院 the Supreme People's Procuratorate
4. 检察职能 procuratorial function
5. 司法保障 judicial guarantee
6. 优质的 quality; high-quality; top-grade
7. 检察机关 procuratorial organ
8. 法治营商环境 business environment based on the rule of law; a legalized setting for business development
9. 深刻践行……理念 persistently uphold and adhere to the concept of... / profoundly understand and unswervingly practice the theory of...
10. 坚持……原则 adhere to / follow / remain committed to the principle of ...
11. 市场主体 market player
12. 整顿和规范 normalization and regulation; rectify and regulate
13. 侵害 hinder; do harm to; encroach on
14. 企业家 entrepreneurs
15. 人身权 personal rights
16. 财产权 property rights
17. 强化监督 intensify supervision
18. 有案不立 do not file cases that should be on file
19. 违法立案 file cases illegally
20. 刑事的 criminal
21. 民事的 civil
22. 审判和执行 trial and enforcement
23. 诉讼欺诈 litigation fraud
24. 法律监督 legal supervision (on ...)

保障法治营商环境建设

建设粤港澳大湾区是习近平总书记亲自谋划、亲自部署、亲自推动的国家战略。2020年3月，最高人民检察院印发《关于充分履行检察职能服务和保障粤港澳大湾区建设的意见》，要求充分发挥检察职能作用，努力为大湾区建设提供高效的法律服务和司法保障。

广东检察机关进一步更新司法理念，深化改革创新，树立国际视野，发挥好各项检察职能，积极探索粤港澳司法交流合作机制，以优质的法治产品、检察产品服务大湾区建设。

一流的湾区建设需要优质的法治营商环境。广东省检察机关深刻践行"法治是最好的营商环境"这一理念，以服务保障民营经济健康发展为切入点，坚持平等保护和全面保护原则，为各类市场主体打造暖心、舒适、健康的营商环境。检察机关积极参与整顿和规范市场经济秩序，依法惩治侵害民营企业和民营企业家人身权、财产权的犯罪行为，为湾区企业发展提供优质高效的司法保障。

强化涉企民事行政诉讼监督，重点监督纠正有案不立、违法立案以及利用刑事手段插手经济纠纷等问题。监督纠正涉及民营企业经济纠纷的审判和执行活动，在全国率先出台对民事诉讼欺诈加强法律监督的指导意见。

为了适应市场经济发展的司法需求,通过召开座谈会、开展检察开放日、送法进企业等方式开通企业与检察院之间的沟通渠道,深入了解湾区企业司法需求,为企业送去更加贴心的菜单式、精准化法律服务,鼓励更多社会主体投身大湾区创新创业。

IV. Extended Terms and Expressions 词汇拓展训练

Directions: *Fill in the following chart and try to get familiar with these extended terms and expressions.*

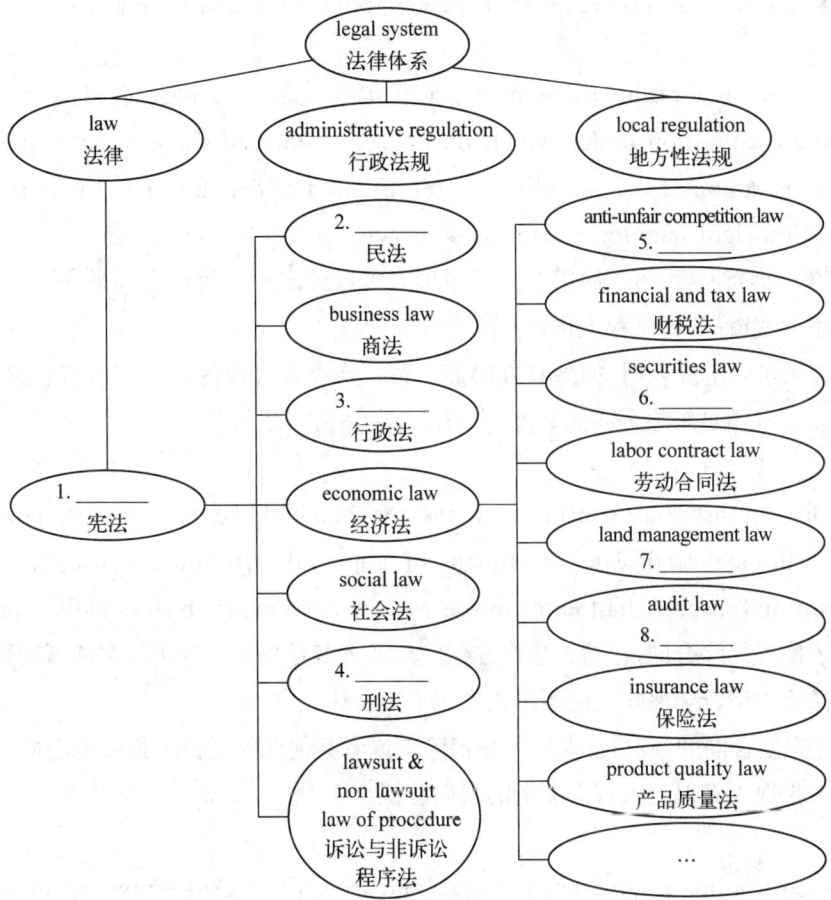

V. Sentence Translation 句子翻译训练

Directions: *Each of the following sentences is followed by two versions of translation. Make a comparison between them and decide which one is better. Then discuss with group members and share your viewpoints.*

1. This law is formulated for the purpose of regulating the insurance activities, protecting the legitimate rights and interests of parties to insurance activities, strengthening the supervision and administration of the insurance sector, maintaining the social and economic order and public interests, and promoting the healthy development of the insurance sector.
   A. 这条法律被制定是为了规范保险活动,保护保险活动当事人的合法权益,加强对保险业的监督管理,维护社会经济秩序和社会公共利益,促进保险事业的健康发展。
   B. 为了规范保险活动,保护保险活动当事人的合法权益,加强对保险业的监督管理,维护社会经济秩序和社会公共利益,促进保险事业的健康发展,制定本法。

2. The parties may terminate a contract if they have so agreed. The parties may prescribe a condition under which one party is entitled to terminate the contract. Upon satisfaction of the condition for termination of the contract, the party with the termination right may terminate the contract.
   A. 当事人协商一致,可以解除合同。当事人可以约定一方解除合同的条件。解除合同的条件成就时,解除权人可以解除合同。
   B. 当事人可以解除合同,如果双方协商一致。当事人可以约定一方有权解除合同的条件。一旦满足解除合同的条件,有解除权的一方可以解除合同。

3. To modify an insurance contract, the insurer shall endorse the insurance policy or any other insurance certificate or attach an approval slip thereto, or the insurance applicant and insurer shall enter into a written agreement on the modification.
   A. 为了修改保险合同,保险人应当在保险单或者其他保险凭证上签名或者附贴批单,或者保险申请者和保险人应当进入变更书面协议。
   B. 变更保险合同的,应当由保险人在保险单或者其他保险凭证上批注或者附贴批单,或者由投保人和保险人订立变更的书面协议。

4. Any listed trading of government bonds and share of securities investment funds shall be governed by the present law. In case there is any special provision in any other law or administrative regulation, such special provision shall prevail.
   A. 政府债券、证券投资基金份额的上市交易,适用本法;其他法律、行政法规另有规定的,适用其规定。
   B. 现有的法律管理政府债券、证券投资基金份额的上市交易。如果其他法律、行政法规有特殊规定,按照这些特殊规定执行。

5. 从事保险活动必须遵守法律、行政法规,尊重社会公德,不得损害社会公共利益。
   A. Whoever carries out the insurance activities must abide by the laws and administrative regulations and defer to the social ethics, and shall not jeopardize the public interests.
   B. While taking part in the insurance activities, we must follow the laws and administrative regulations and respect the social public moralities, and must not harm the public interests.

6. 债权人可以拒绝债务人部分履行债务,但部分履行不损害债权人利益的除外。债务人部分履行债务给债权人增加的费用,由债务人承担。
   A. An obligee is able to refuse the debtor's part of fulfillment, but such part of fulfillment without harming the obligee's interests is not included. If the debtor's part of fulfillment causes extra cost for the obligee, then the debtor should pay for the expense.
   B. An obligee may reject the obligor's partial performance, except where such partial performance does not harm the obligee's interests. Any additional expense incurred by the obligee due to the obligor's partial performance shall be borne by the obligor.

7. 证券发行、交易活动的当事人具有平等的法律地位,应当遵守自愿、有偿、诚实信用的原则。
   A. The parties of any issuance or transaction of securities shall have equal legal status and shall obey the principles of free will, compensation and honesty and creditworthiness.
   B. Anyone joining issuance or transaction of securities enjoys equal legal status and should follow the principles of being willing, being paid and being honest and trustworthy.

8. 为了加强土地管理,维护土地的社会主义公有制,保护、开发土地资源,合理利用土地,切实保护耕地,促进社会经济的可持续发展,根据宪法,制定本法。
   A. This law is formulated in accordance with the Constitution in order to strengthen land administration, uphold the socialist public ownership of land, protect and develop land resources, ensure a rational use of land, give a real protection to cultivated land, and promote sustainable development of socialist economy.
   B. In order to increase land control, keep the socialist public land ownership, protect and develop land resources, use land rationally, effectively protect the farm land,

and realize sustainable development of socialist economy, according to the Constitution to draft this law.

Ⅵ. Abstract Translation 摘要翻译训练

Directions: *Go through the list of terminologies and get familiar with these terms. Then try to translate the following abstract into English and learn how to write an abstract in a proper way.*

Terminologies
1. 法律制度 legal system
2. 房产税 housing property tax
3. 制止，束缚；控制；约束；遏制 curb
4. 投机买卖；投机活动 speculation
5. 土地出让金 land transfer fund
6. 制定法律 enact law
7. 不动产 real estate
8. 房产评估 property assessment

我国个人住房房产税法律制度的构建

摘要： 开征个人住房房产税可以提高住房持有成本，直接遏制住房投机，对抑制高房价有重要作用。个人住房房产税还可以提供稳定的地方财政来源，促进社会财富公平分配。我国应当构建个人住房房产税法律制度，处理好个人住房房产税与土地出让金的关系，实行"高保有、低流转"的房地产税制，制定统一的《房产税法》。我国还应当建立不动产统一登记法律制度、完善房产评估法律制度，为个人住房房产税全面征收提供条件。

关键词： 高房价；个人住房房产税；法律制度

Ⅶ. Academic Debate 学术思辨训练

Directions: *Read the following topic and try to translate the provided viewpoints. Then have a discussion with your group members and find more support for both sides. Hold an English debate in class between two groups. Remember: your arguments can refer to but are not limited to the points provided.*

🎤 **Debate Topic**   Solicitors should prioritize the interests of their clients rather than those of the nation.

Pros:
1. 律师靠打赢官司赢得声誉,靠声誉在业界立足,只有尽全力帮助自己的当事人打赢官司,才能与当事人达到"双赢"的完美状态。
2. 如在办案过程中知悉当事人的违法行为,则不予维护,但也不能揭发。
3. 如发现当事人的违法行为正在实施或即将实施,要进行劝阻或劝其自首,但不准举报。
4. 从根本上说,律师的职业责任和职业道德就是尽最大可能维护当事人的利益,帮助当事人打赢官司。

Cons:
1. 律师只是当事人利益的"独联体",而并非当事人利益的"共同体"。可见,律师不是当事人"花钱雇佣的枪手"。
2. 如果无视公正原则和正义立场,即使帮助当事人打赢了官司,律师也会惨遭世人痛骂,更要遭到自身良心的谴责。
3. 律师辩护的是"当事人的合法权益",而不能简单地理解为"当事人的利益"。如果利欲熏心、藐视法律、不讲原则,一心只求为当事人脱罪,甚至不惜歪曲事实、捏造舆论、无所不用其极,势必极大威胁法律秩序和社会稳定,这就不仅触及职业道德,而且涉嫌违法。
4. 从根本上说,律师是法治社会和公平正义的象征,律师的职业责任和职业道德就是捍卫国家法律和社会正义。

Ⅷ. Theoretical Guidance 翻译理论指导

笔译技巧:语序转换

英汉两大语言在句子基本结构上存在明显差异。英汉互译过程中如果受制于原文语言结构和表达方式的束缚,就容易导致行文不通顺,严重损害译文质量。因此,为了避免"翻译腔",译者往往需要对原文的语序加以调整。具体处理手段包括主谓结构的重新确定,在主语、谓语、定语、宾语、状语、补语等句子成分之间进行语序转换以及各类从句的转换。总之,语序转换即根据原文内容和逻辑关系,分解源语句子的各个成分,按照译入语的句子结构和表达习惯重新安排句子各成分的顺序。

请结合笔译技巧解析视频,完成下列句子翻译,注意巧用语序转换技巧。

英译汉练习:

1. **There is something in Christmas which appeals to all of us**, namely warmth, love, care, union, harmony and dedication.

2. We have also taped **information about how to apply for a visa that people can get by telephoning the embassy for instructions**.

3. We know that a cat, **whose eyes can take in many more rays of light than human eyes**, can see clearly in the night.

4. I do not believe in **fate that falls on us no matter what we do**, but, I do believe in **fate that will fall on us if we do nothing**.

汉译英练习:

1. <u>正是由于</u>人类拥有复杂的大脑,我们<u>才</u>能够开展各种复杂的思维活动。

2. 会议推迟应该由他负责,<u>这是个无法改变的事实</u>。

3. <u>与其说</u>军队重视纪律,<u>不如说</u>军队更重视自律。

4. <u>他们企图扑灭反抗,结果徒劳一场,反抗越来越猛烈,遍及全国。</u>

Chapter 5　Cultural & Creative Design
文 创 设 计

Ⅰ. Academic Background 学术背景汇报

Directions: *Study the following questions before class and try to search for some relevant information. Then discuss these questions with your group members. Give a brief introduction to the discipline of design and present it in class.*

1. What are the sub-disciplines of design?
2. What key factors lead to successful cultural and creative design?
3. Can you name a few well-known cultural and creative designs both at home and abroad?
4. What is your favorite cultural and creative design? why do you like it?

Ⅱ. E-C Academic Translation 英汉学术翻译

Directions: *Study the notes in advance. Then read the following passage carefully and translate it into Chinese with the help of the notes supplied. Try to enrich your academic vocabulary and sentence patterns.*

1. co-founder　　*n*. 联合发起人；共同创立者
2. along with　与……一起；伴随
3. the (vast) majority of　大多数
4. inspire　*v*. 激励；鼓舞；赋予灵感
5. feel identified　获得认同
6. in honor of　为了纪念……
7. initial　*adj*. 最初的；开始的
8. blonde　*n*. 金发女郎　*adj*. 金发碧眼的
9. zebra printed　斑马纹的
10. eternal　*adj*. 不朽的；永恒的
11. masculine　*adj*. 男子汉的；阳刚的
12. name after　以……命名
13. commercial　*adj*. 贸易的；商业的
    commercialize *v*. 商业化
14. pony　*n*. 矮马；小马
15. vital　*adj*. 必不可少的；对……极重要的
16. up-to-date　*adj*. 最新(式)的；时髦的
17. hand-painted　*adj*. 手绘的
18. catwalk　*n*. T 台；猫步

19. sophisticated *adj*. 见多识广的；老于世故的
20. stir up 搅拌；煽动；激起
21. exorbitant *adj*. 过高的；高得离谱的
22. icon *n*. 偶像；图标；圣像
23. obsession *n*. 痴迷；困扰；着魔
    be obsessed with 对……着迷

Forever Barbie

Barbie is the most famous doll in the whole planet. Who doesn't know her? Her real name is Barbara Millicent Roberts, and her first introduction to the public took place on March 9th 1959, at the Toy Fair in New York. She was created by Ruth Handler, co-founder of the toy company Mattel, along with her husband Elliot Handler.

In the 50s, Ruth realized her daughter would rather play with dolls that looked like adults, more than with childish ones. Her kid would spend hours dressing and undressing cut-out dolls. At that time, the vast majority of dolls out in the market had the physical appearance of children. When she realized about the idea of business she had in mind, she thought it would be a good idea to create a doll that looked young. However, this idea didn't convince her business partner and husband.

During a trip around Europe, they discovered a popular Dutch doll called Lilli. It was a doll inspired by cartoons for adults. Mattel bought the rights for Lilli, stopped its production and started making Ruth's doll. They wanted to offer girls a different doll, adapting to the social changes that women were starting to experiment, and with which young girls could feel identified. The name they chose was Barbie, in honor of Barbara, the Handler's daughter. After her first appearance at the Toy Fair, the market's response was amazing. Even the company had some initial problems to be able to provide all the dolls they were asked for!

The first Barbie had a blonde hair, very fashionable with a zebra printed swimsuit. Barbie was not alone for long. Throughout the years, some more characters have been added to her life. Apart from plenty of friends, she also has some younger sisters. The most famous ones are Kelly, Chelsea and Stacy, all between 10 and 13 years old. Also, Ken is right next to her, her eternal boyfriend. The masculine version of Barbie was named after Kenneth, the Handler's son.

Since her first stage as a teenager model, Barbie has had plenty of different jobs. She's been a dentist, a gymnast, a teacher, a dancer, a photographer, a vet, a doctor, a singer, an astronaut, a flight attendant, a president, a pilot … Yes, she has a pilot license, and she can fly commercial aircraft. She loves animals and she's had more than

40 pet dogs, horses, cats, parrots ...

Behind every Barbie, there is a group of five hundred specialists that work at the Mattel research and development center, in Los Angeles. Technology and design are vital for its manufacturing process, where they combine the most up-to-date techniques with traditional methods. The manufacturing process of a Barbie is not easy. The body is shaped by the plastic injection system, while her face is hand-painted and her hair is set with a sewing machine. Once the head is fixed to the body, it's time for the hair cut and hair do. Her dresses are also sewed by hand. The Mattel designers visit the most important catwalks of the world to keep up with every season's collections.

Just like our society, Barbie's image has been evolving throughout the years. Back in the beginning, she had unreal measurements and her face was serious and sophisticated. She's been gaining mobility and changes in her body to adapt to the new times. Her waist is wider now, her breast is smaller, and she's been adopting a more natural and relaxed aspect. With the idea of having more little girls feeling identified with the doll, during 2016, Mattel introduced a new collection that stirred half world up. With more realistic measurements and sizes, Fashionista Barbies appeared, including different body types, skin colors, eye colors and hair does.

Barbie is the best-seller among doll history, while Mattel rapidly rises to be one of the 20 most valued brands in the world as well as ranks number one among the world of toys. Commercialization has been promoted in more than 140 countries and the estimation comes that two Barbies are sold every minute. Collecting toys has become a very popular hobby, particularly collecting Barbies. Every year, more than 100 different models of Barbie are created, including her family and friends. There are also a lot of special editions with exorbitant prices.

With more than 50 years of history, Barbie has achieved dreams almost impossible to believe for a doll. Barbie is not only a doll; she is a fashion and social icon. Her popularity has never stopped growing and it seems like the Barbie obsession has NO END!

Ⅲ. C-E Academic Translation 汉英学术翻译

Directions: *Study the notes in advance. Then read the following passage carefully and translate it into English with the help of the notes supplied. Try to enrich your academic vocabulary and sentence patterns.*

1. 美国邮政总局 the United States Postal Service
2. 发行 issue;release;distribute
3. 庆祝 celebrate;commemorate
4. 绘图艺术家 graphic artist
5. 家喻户晓 a household name;be known to every household
6. 享誉全球;扬名四海 be recognized around the world;be internationally recognized;enjoy international fame
7. 繁忙的 busy;bustling;rush
8. 描绘 describe;portray;depict
9. 打动人心的 touching;heart-wrenching;appealing;moving
10. 鸡年 the Year of the Rooster
11. 销售一空 be sold out;buy up
12. 畅销 sell well;best-seller;big hit;be in great demand;have a ready market for products;be much in demand on the market
13. 委托 commission;entrust
14. 属相;生肖 Chinese Zodiac symbol/sign
15. 体现 demonstrate;incorporate;embody;contain
16. 引人注目的 eye-catching;striking;remarkable
17. 联合发行 joint issue
18. 以……为特色 feature;be characterized by
19. 黑颈鹤 a black-necked crane
20. 引吭高歌的鹤 a whooping crane
21. 广岛 Hiroshima
22. 成名的原因 claim to fame

设计中的文化元素

美国邮政总局近日发行庆祝2008年北京奥运的新邮票。这套邮票是由一位夏威夷的华裔绘图艺术家设计的。这位艺术家虽然不能算是家喻户晓,可是他设计的邮票却享誉全球。

正午时分,檀香山邮局里业务非常繁忙。顾客余珍正在购买一整版的奥运纪念邮票:"我觉得邮票真的很棒,我很喜欢。不仅颜色很漂亮,而且展示了动态的体操运动员。"余女士也惊喜地发现,这张邮票是夏威夷著名艺术设计师克拉伦斯·李的作品。邮票以鲜红的色彩描绘出一名跳跃中的体操选手。据李声称,这样的设计是为了弘扬奥运精神:"这个画面充满活力,打动人心,富有动感。"

克拉伦斯·李可不是头一次设计邮票。美国邮政总局在1992年就请他设计了一套以华裔美国人为主题的新年邮票。当时鸡年展望在际,李早已胸有成竹。他的鸡年邮票不仅在美国很受欢迎,在中国也深受喜爱,总销售额高达500万美元。美国邮政总局为之震惊,显然他们当初并不知道中国有两千万集邮爱好者。由于这是第一枚描绘中国特色形象、以中国剪纸艺术为题材的美国邮票,并且大胆运用了中国风色彩调配方案,且推广工作很成功,邮票很快便被销售一空。由于鸡年邮票如此畅销,美国邮政总局委托李再设计一套十二属相的邮票。据李所述,他最喜欢猪年邮票,图案中的小猪在空中飞翔,看起来非常快乐、生动。

　　现如今，由于设计了诸多融合文化元素的邮票，李已经扬名国际。李曾为夏威夷和世界各地的大公司设计过引人注目的商标图案，以及特殊活动的文宣海报。1994年，李设计了第一套美国和中国联合发行的邮票。这套邮票共两枚，设计特色是一只黑颈鹤和一只引吭高歌的鹤。有人问李如果现在又要他设计一套邮票的话，他会选用什么主题？他毫不犹豫地回答："我会选择世界和平。"

　　克拉伦斯·李今年已经七十开外，他继续从事艺术设计和创作。使他感到惊奇的是，让他名扬四海的作品竟然是他最小的设计——邮票。

Ⅳ. Extended Terms and Expressions 词汇拓展训练

Directions: *Fill in the following chart and try to get familiar with these extended terms and expressions.*

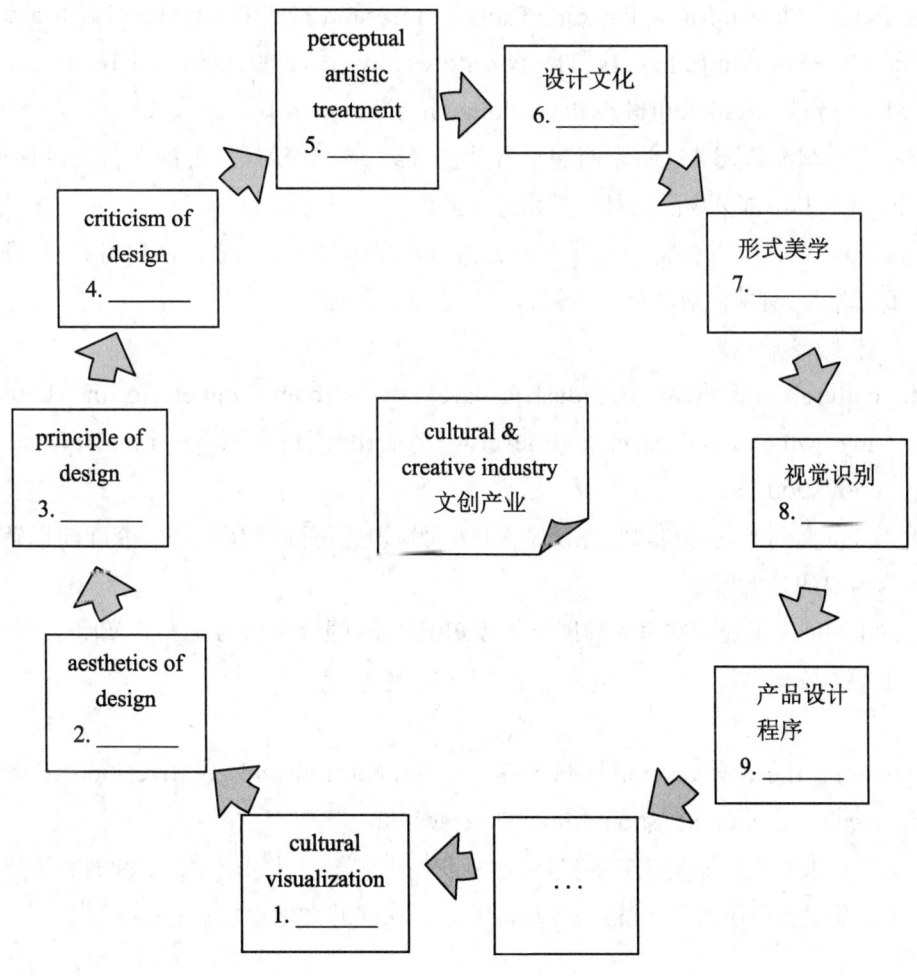

Ⅴ. Sentence Translation 句子翻译训练

Directions: *Each of the following sentences is followed by two versions of translation. Make a comparison between them and decide which one is better. Then discuss with group members and share your viewpoints.*

1. By the end of 2020, the Palace Museum has created 9,170 cultural and creative products and the revenue coming from sales of such products in 2016 surpassed 1 billion yuan.

    A. 2020年年底,故宫创造了9 170件文创产品,来自这些产品的收入2020年超过10亿元。

    B. 截至2020年年底,故宫开发的文创产品达9 170件,本年度文创产品销售收入超过10亿元。

2. The Palace Museum now has one Taobao store and one Tmall store with a total of around 3.66 million followers. The two stores have over 500 products for sale, several of which registered monthly sales volume of more than 10,000.

    A. 故宫在淘宝和天猫这两家网购平台共拥有约366万粉丝。目前在售商品种类超过500款,其中部分商品的月销量超过1万件。

    B. 故宫现在有一个淘宝店、一个天猫店和366万左右的追随者。两店有超过500件的商品出售,有些注册商品的月销售总量超过1万件。

3. The cultural and creative industries are now strongly linked to the knowledge economy, which emphasizes high levels of research, knowledge transfer, and above all, innovation.

    A. 当今的文创产业与知识经济紧密关联,而知识经济强调高水平研究和知识转化,最为重要的是强调创新。

    B. 文化和创新工业现在很大程度上依赖知识经济,强调研究的高水平、知识传播和创新也很重要。

4. In pursuing the new economic benefits of the cultural and creative industries, their deeper cultural contexts should not be neglected.

    A. 为了追求文创产业实现新的经济效益,我们不应忽视其深层次的文化背景因素。

    B. 在追求文创产业的新经济效益过程中,它们深层的文化背景不应被忽视。

5. 店里出售各种主题的胶带、手包、手机壳等商品，主题包括罗塞塔石碑、埃及木乃伊等。
   A. The store sells tapes, handbags, mobile phone shells and other items with various themes such as the Rosetta stone, Egyptian mummy and so on.
   B. Various themes products such as tape, handbag and hand-phone shell are on sale, and the themes include the Rosetta stone and Egyptian mummy.

6. 最近几年，随着政府加大对文创产业的大力支持，人们愈发热衷于博物馆的"副业"。
   A. Recently, with strong government support for the cultural and creative industries, people are more and more interested in museums' "side business".
   B. In recent years, as the government attaches greater support to cultural and creative industries, people become increasingly crazy with the "side business" of museums.

7. 首批发售的 20 款文化产品中，15 款已经暂时售罄。
   A. Of the first 20 cultural products on sale, 15 have been temporarily out of store.
   B. The store initially launched 20 items of cultural products, 15 of which have been temporarily sold out.

8. 7 月 1 日，"全球四大博物馆"之一的大英博物馆在天猫平台开设旗舰店。
   A. The British Museum, one of the "four major museums in the world", opened its flagship store on Tmall on July 1.
   B. July 1, one of the "four great global museums" the British Museum set up its flag shop on the Tmall platform.

Ⅵ. Abstract Translation 摘要翻译训练

Directions: *Go through the list of terminologies and get familiar with these terms. Then try to translate the following abstract into English and learn how to write an abstract in a proper way.*

Terminologies
1. 少数民族 ethnic minority
2. 达翰尔族 Daur nationality
3. 敦厚质朴的 pure and honest; unsophisticated
4. 榆木 elm
5. 松木 pine
6. 桦木 birch
7. 杨木 poplar wood
8. 柳木 willow

少数民族文创产品的开发研究

摘要：由于长期以来居住处偏远地区，我国嫩江流域少数民族与外界交流不便，因此发展并沿袭了独特、自然、淳朴的文化。本课题研究两个具有代表性的民族——达翰尔族和满族的传统材料（例如牛、羊、鹿、马、鱼等动物的皮、角、毛、牙等以及榆木、松木、桦木、杨木、柳木等植物的茎、秆、根、皮等），加工工艺及技术创新，帮助我们更好地了解并传承文化设计，使之成为现代文创产品设计点的灵感源泉。

关键词：达翰尔族；满族；文创产品；设计

Ⅶ. Academic Debate 学术思辨训练

Directions: *Read the following topic and try to translate the provided viewpoints. Then have a discussion with your group members and find more support for both sides. Hold an English debate in class between two groups. Remember：your arguments can refer to but are not limited to the points provided.*

Debate Topic Nowadays, it is a creative idea to set up souvenir shops at the exit of exhibitions and tourist attractions, which can bring us more nice memories of our visit.

Pros：
1. 游客除了拍照留念，还可以自行挑选购买一些很有特色的文创产品，这些都能为参观与旅行增添不少乐趣。
2. 文创产品往往设计精致，造型优美，寓意深远，其本身就是一种艺术创作，具有很高的艺术价值和收藏价值。
3. 展馆或旅游景点推出文创纪念品商店有助于传承文化、宣扬文化，使游客了解相关的文化知识，也有助于向外国友人传递文化的魅力。
4. 现今许多博物馆都免费开发，出售一些文创产品，既能够满足游客留念的需求，又能够为博物馆的进一步建设筹集一部分经费。

Cons:
1. 纪念品商品往往价格虚高,标价远远超出商品的实际价值,商家借机谋取暴利。
2. 有些文创产品并非独家设计经营的,以次充好,在网上随时都能够买到,消费者高价购买之后发现自己有上当受骗之嫌。
3. 很多博物馆和旅游景点把文创纪念品店安排在出口的必经之路上,诱导或迫使游客进入商店,这其实是很不可取的,降低了游客的旅游体验感。
4. 有些博物馆和旅游景点在进入文创商店或购买文创商品时还要求游客下载相关 app 或关注指定微信公众号,这种行为也侵害了游客的权益。

Ⅷ. Theoretical Guidance 翻译理论指导

笔译技巧:语态转换

　　主动语态的典型表达形式为"主语+谓语+宾语",英汉被动语态的典型表达形式分别为 be done 和"被……"。但在翻译过程中的语态处理是一个复杂的问题,切忌千篇一律地将源语中的语态形式照搬至译入语中。众所周知,出于"受事方是谈话的主题或中心""施事方不明或无说明之必要""出于某种考虑故意不提施事方"或"语篇内部的衔接"等考虑,英语被动语态使用频率较高,尤其是英语的科技文本和政府公文等正式语体更加倾向于使用被动语态。而汉语则不然,这是因为汉语中有相当一部分被动的意义可以通过非典型被动句甚至主动句的形式予以表达。因此,英汉互译要注意从语义角度出发,灵活处理语态之间的转换,尊重译文读者的语言表达习惯,着眼译文通顺。

> 请结合笔译技巧解析视频,完成下列句子翻译,注意巧用语态转换技巧。

英译汉练习:

1. Vitamin C **is destroyed** when it **is overheated**.

2. The Y-rays **are not affected by** an electric field.

3. It **is universally known** that the world **is made up of** matter.

4. The English language **is being destroyed by** a "deadly virus of management speak", which has infected the mouths and minds of politicians like Tony Blair and George W. Bush.

 汉译英练习:

1. 这件事必须在适当的时候用适当的手段**予以处理**。

2. 我国各族人民都要热烈**庆祝**"十一"国庆节。

3. 上周日,来访的客人**和陪同人员一起参观了**黄鹤楼。

4. 面试时**总共问了**十个问题,他表现出色,**给**所有的面试官**留下了**极其深刻的**印象**。

Chapter 6　Biochemical Engineering

生 化 工 程

Ⅰ. Academic Background 学术背景汇报

irections: *Study the following questions before class and try to search for some relevant information. Then discuss these questions with your group members. Give a brief introduction to the discipline of biochemical engineering and present it in class.*

1. What is biochemical engineering?
2. Can you name some branches of biochemical engineering?
3. Do you know the origin of biochemical industry?
4. Why is biochemical engineering important in our life? Give examples.

Ⅱ. E-C Academic Translation 英汉学术翻译

irections: *Study the notes in advance. Then read the following passage carefully and translate it into Chinese with the help of the notes supplied. Try to enrich your academic vocabulary and sentence patterns.*

1. sarin　*n*. 沙林毒气
2. fast-acting　快速作用的;快速反应的
3. toxic　*adj*. 有毒的
   toxin　*n*. 毒素
4. agent　*n*. 化学剂;药剂
5. potent　*adj*. 强有力的;强效的
6. release　*n*./*v*. 释放
7. pose risk to　对……造成威胁
8. odor　*n*. 气味
   odorless　*adj*. 无气味的
9. evaporate　*v*. 蒸发
10. volatile　*adj*. 易变的;易挥发的
    volatility　*n*. 挥发性

11. massacre　*n*./*v*. 屠杀;杀戮
12. civilian　*n*. 平民;老百姓
13. terrorist attack　恐怖袭击
    terrorism　*n*. 恐怖主义
14. corrode　*v*. 腐蚀;侵蚀
    corrosive　*adj*. 腐蚀性的;侵蚀性的
    corrosion　*n*. 腐蚀;侵蚀
15. resist　*v*. 抵抗;抵挡;使……不受伤害
16. drool　*v*. 流口水
17. vomit　*v*. 呕吐
18. diarrhea　*n*. 腹泻
19. symptom　*n*. 症状
20. consume　*v*. 消费;消耗

consumption *n*. 摄入；消耗
21. convulsion   *n*. 抽搐；痉挛
22. paralysis   *n*. 麻痹；瘫痪
23. respiratory   *adj*. 呼吸的
24. dose   *n*. 剂量
25. disperse   *v*. 驱散；散开；传播
26. contaminate   *v*. 污染；弄脏
    contamination *n*. 污染；污秽
27. antidote   *n*. 解药
28. counteract   *v*. 抵消；抵抗；中和
29. neurological   *adj*. 神经系统的；神经（病）学的

Chemical Weapons — Sarin

Sarin, a man-made, fast-acting and highly toxic nerve agent, was originally developed in Germany in 1938 to be used as a pesticide. But according to the U.S. Centers for Disease Control and Prevention (CDC), it is far more potent. Sarin can be mixed in liquid to poison drinking water and food, or released as a gas, where it may pose greater risk to a larger number of people.

Victims generally have no idea when they're being exposed. Sarin is a clear, odorless, colorless and tasteless liquid that evaporates at about the same rate as water when released, making it one of the more volatile nerve agents. It was used in the 1988 Halabja massacre, in which Saddam Hussein ordered the release of sarin gas over the Kurdish city and killed at least 5,000 civilians over three days, as well as in a Tokyo subway terrorist attack in 1995 that killed 13 people. Its volatility means sarin is generally mixed just before it's used and, once made, stored in liquid form. Sarin is also highly corrosive and needs to be stored in specially designed containers that resist breakdown.

Within a few seconds of sarin-gas exposure, victims will start to experience eye pain, drooling, weakness, vomiting, diarrhea and irregular heart rates. Clothing from victims exposed to the gas will continue to release toxic vapors for 30 minutes, causing more people to come into contact with it. For those exposed to the liquid form of sarin, symptoms can occur anytime from a few minutes to 18 hours after consumption. If exposed to a large amount of sarin in either gas or liquid form, victims can experience more severe and painful symptoms such as convulsions, paralysis, loss of respiratory functions and even death.

If only exposed to a small dose, most people can recover. Health officials recommend moving to an outdoor area if exposed indoors, in order to disperse the gas and lower the dose of exposure. Removing contaminated clothing as quickly as possible and washing exposed areas with soap and water can also reduce risk of more severe symptoms. If exposed patients are treated immediately with an antidote that counteracts the toxin in a hospital, the CDC says they will likely survive without neurological problems lasting more than one to two weeks. However, severe and untreated exposure is likely to result in death, making sarin one of the most potent nerve agents.

III. C-E Academic Translation 汉英学术翻译

Directions: *Study the notes in advance. Then read the following passage carefully and translate it into English with the help of the notes supplied. Try to enrich your academic vocabulary and sentence patterns.*

1. 原油 crude; crude oil
2. 分馏 fractionate; fractionation
3. 蒸馏 distill; distillation
4. 互溶的液体 mutually soluble liquids
5. 沸点 boiling point
6. 进料 feed; feedstock
7. 汽化 vaporize; vaporization
8. 塔顶产品 overhead product
9. 塔底产品 bottom product
10. 组成;成分 composition; constituent
11. 石油提炼厂 petroleum refinery
12. 蒸馏釜 still; distilling still
13. 冷凝 condense; condensation
14. 轻馏分 light fraction
15. 重馏分 heavy fraction
16. 生产 yield; produce
17. 指定的;特定的 specified
18. 精馏 rectify; rectification
19. 扩散 diffusion; spread
20. 单程的 single-stage
21. 双程的 double-stage
22. 直燃(式) direct-fired
23. 管式加热器 tubular heater
24. 管式蒸馏釜 pipe still; tube still
25. 常压 atmospheric pressure
26. 真空 vacuum

原油分馏

蒸馏是将互溶的液体根据其沸点(或者更准确的说是沸点范围)的不同通过物理方法分离成各个组分或成分的操作过程。在这一过程中,进料升温到沸点并部分汽化——该过程产生了一个塔顶产品和一个塔底产品,两者在组成上均与进料不同。在现有的石油提炼厂中,蒸馏是在蒸馏釜中进行一次简单蒸馏完成的。这种蒸馏方法会使低沸点的成分变成气相,且停留在蒸馏釜中,这就会降低高沸点成分气化时需要的分压。因而,此操作可在低温下进行。

带有蒸汽冷凝的简单蒸馏可产生一个轻馏分和一个重馏分。轻馏分中低沸点的成分比进料要高,而重馏分中低沸点的成分比进料要低。换句话说,一个馏分中低沸点成分增大,而另一个馏分中高沸点成分增加。但是,对原油进行简单蒸馏无法得到理想的产品,也无法生产某一特定沸点区间的产品。正因为如此,在简单蒸馏之后还需进行精馏。

精馏是一种传质扩散操作,其目的是按沸点的不同分离液体混合物,使用的方法则是使蒸汽和液体反复逆向接触。

原油分馏系统可以是单程的,也可以是双程的,由直燃式炉型管式加热器,即管式蒸馏釜,提供所需热量。而且该分馏系统可在常压或真空条件下操作,这取决于整座工厂的布局设计和需要精馏的原油品质。有时,一个原油分馏系统可能将常压操作和真空操作结合起来。

Ⅳ. Extended Terms and Expressions 词汇拓展训练

Directions: Fill in the following chart and try to get familiar with these extended terms and expressions.

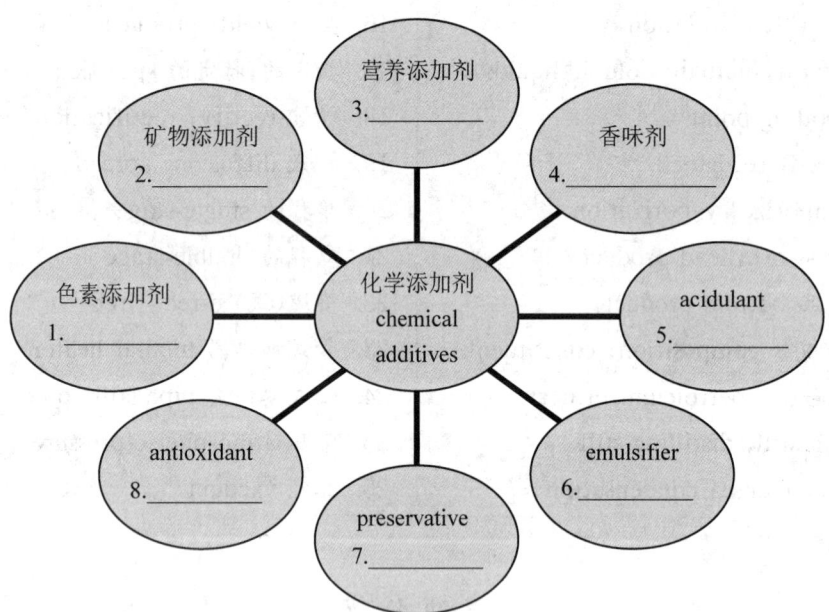

Ⅴ. Sentence Translation 句子翻译训练

Directions: Each of the following sentences is followed by two versions of translation. Make a comparison between them and decide which one is better. Then discuss with group members and share your viewpoints.

1. The explosive growth in petrochemicals in the 1960s and 1970s was largely due to the enormous increase in demand for synthetic polymers such as polyethylene,

polypropylene, nylon, polyesters and epoxy resins.
   A. 20世纪六七十年代,人们对诸如聚乙烯、聚丙烯、尼龙、聚脂纤维和环氧树脂等合成高聚物的需求量大幅上升,进而引发了一场石油化工业的黄金发展期。
   B. 石油化工在1960年代和1970年代期间爆炸性的发展,主要是由于对聚乙烯、聚丙烯、尼龙、聚脂纤维和环氧树脂等合成高聚物的需求的增加而造成的。

2. It has been generally recognized that the synthesis of carbohydrate is dependent on the presence of light, the green substance chlorophyll and a supply of carbon dioxide and water, together with other factors that probably affect the rate of synthesis but do not actually control it.
   A. 通常被认为碳水化合物的合成依赖光、绿色物质叶绿素以及二氧化碳和水的存在,还有一些其他因素可能影响合成速度但事实上并不参与控制。
   B. 一般认为,碳水化合物的合成取决于光照、绿色物质叶绿素以及一定量的二氧化碳和水。其他因素对合成速度也有影响,但无决定作用。

3. DNA can be defined as a kind of chemical, which is located at the center of the cells of living things, with the functions of controlling the structure and purpose of each cell and carrying genetic information during reproduction.
   A. DNA可以被定义为一种位于生命体细胞中心,具有控制每一个细胞的结构和目的、在繁殖过程中承载遗传信息的作用的化学物质。
   B. 脱氧核糖核酸可定义为一种化学物质。该物质位于生命体细胞中心,其作用表现为控制细胞的生长结构和活动目的,并在其繁殖过程中携带遗传信息。

4. Shirts, dresses and suits made from polyesters like Terylene and polyamides like Nylon are crease-resistant, machine-washable, and drip-dry or non-iron. They are also cheaper than natural materials.
   A. 用聚脂(如涤纶)或聚酰胺(如尼龙)所制成的衬衫、裙子和上衣具有抗皱、可机洗、晒干自挺或免烫等优点,同时也比天然面料更便宜。
   B. 衬衫、裙子和上衣采用聚脂(如涤纶)或聚酰胺(如尼龙)为原料,则可抗皱、可机洗、晒干自挺或免烫。它们也比天然面料更便宜。

5. 这些材料用来制造消费品,令我们的生活更加舒适便捷,比如生产的医药制品能够帮助人类维护健康,甚至维持生命。
   A. These materials are used to produce consumer products, which may bring more comfort and convenience to our life, in some cases such as pharmaceutical

products that help to maintain our well-being or even life itself.

B. We use these materials to produce commodities and make our life comfortable and convenient, for example, the medicine production helps humans to maintain health or life.

6. 从体育跑道、足球场和网球场的全天候人造篷顶,到球拍的尼龙线,还有完全由合成材料制成的高尔夫球和足球,可见塑料和高聚物的应用对休闲活动产生很重要的影响。

   A. Ranging from all-weather man-made umbrellas for running lanes, football and tennis fields to nylon strings for rackets, golf balls and footballs made totally from synthetic materials, it is obvious that it is very important to apply plastics and polymers in recreation.

   B. Apparently, applications of plastics and polymers greatly affect leisure activities from all-weather artificial surfaces for athletic tracks, football pitches and tennis courts to nylon strings for rackets and items like golf balls and footballs made entirely from synthetic materials.

7. 干细胞除了可以累积并保存这些致癌突变,还具有强大的增殖能力,因而成为癌化的理想目标。

   A. In addition to accumulating and preserving these oncogenic scars, a stem cell's enormous proliferative capacity makes it an ideal target for malignancy.

   B. A stem cell can accumulate and keep these cancer mutation. It also has enormous reproductive ability and becomes an ideal target for cancer.

8. 这种企业经营的国际化格局,即全球化,是化工业的一大发展趋势。大公司通过在其他国家开办工厂或收购现有的工厂进行扩张。

   A. Such international framework for operations is called globalization, which is a developing trend for the chemical industry. Some big companies enlarge their activities by establishing factories in other countries or by purchasing existing factories.

   B. This international outlook for operations, or globalization, is a growing trend within the chemical industry, with large-scale companies expanding their business either by erecting manufacturing units in other countries or by taking over companies which are already operating there.

Ⅵ. Abstract Translation 摘要翻译训练

Directions: *Go through the list of terminologies and get familiar with these terms. Then try to translate the following abstract into English and learn how to write an abstract in a proper way.*

Terminologies
1. 图位克隆 map-based cloning
2. 功能克隆 functional cloning
3. 表型克隆 phonetypical cloning
4. 分子标记 molecular marker
5. 基因组文库 genome library
6. 遗传系统 heredity system
7. 多型现象 pleomorphism
8. 染色体步移 chromosome walking

植物基因分离的图位克隆技术

摘要：传统的基因功能克隆、表型克隆方法具有基因表达产物不清楚，难以进行相关基因分离等缺点。目前，图位克隆技术日渐成熟，已成为分离基因的有效方法，并在分离不同的植物基因中得到了广泛的应用。本文简要介绍图位克隆技术原理，并详细阐述图位克隆操作的四个重要技术环节：筛选与目的基因紧密连锁的分子标记、目的基因的定位、构建高质量容易操作的大片段基因组文库和目的基因的筛选和鉴定。本文还概述了近年来利用图位克隆技术分离植物基因的研究成果以及最新研究进展，并对图位技术的应用前景做出展望：在不久的将来，在基因组学中遗传系统理论的指导下，在具有高多态性水平的分子标记的背景下，应用图位克隆技术在植物基因克隆研究中必将取得更加辉煌的成果。

关键词：图位克隆；分子标记；定位；染色体步移

Ⅶ. Academic Debate 学术思辨训练

Directions: *Read the following topic and try to translate the provided viewpoints. Then have a discussion with your group members and find more support for both sides. Hold an English debate in class between two groups. Remember: your arguments can refer to but are not limited to the points provided.*

Debate Topic   Transgenic creatures and transgenic food should be encouraged to thrive so as to protect the diversity of creatures as well as alleviate famine around the world.

Pros：

1. 移植动植物基因并将其加以改变，可以改良动植物的某种特性，例如把某些细菌的基因接入玉米、大豆等植株，可以更好地保护植株不受害虫的侵害。
2. 转基因技术可以帮助人类培育更高产、抗病虫害能力更强的优良作物品种，其外表、口感和天然作物没有多大区别，甚至味道更佳，有助于缓解世界粮食短缺问题。
3. 转基因生物不仅产量高，而且成本低廉。有数据显示，转基因食品比同类天然食品的价格低20%～30%。
4. 世界头号经济强国美国是转基因技术发展最快的国家，其国内转基因作物品种最多，种植面积最大，美国公众接收转基因食品的程度也最高。
5. 转基因生物的相关研究将有助于帮助一些濒临灭绝的物种增强生存能力和繁殖能力，进而有助于保护地球的生物多样性。

Cons：

1. 人类通过几千年自身实践所选择的食品已相对固定，转基因生物的出现从根本上动摇了这一基础。转基因生物可能对食品安全、农业安全和生态安全等造成威胁。
2. 转基因食品来自实验室，是通过人工手段制造出来的。这种"异类"食品可能存在安全隐患，因此引起了公众对转基因食品安全性的怀疑。
3. 英国科学家的实验表明，用转基因马铃薯饲养的老鼠出现生长发育受阻、体重减轻、免疫系统遭破坏等六大生理缺陷。
4. 美国科学家指出，抗虫玉米的花粉含有毒素，农田益虫吃了这种花粉或沾有花粉的菜叶后，死亡率显著增高。
5. 丹麦科学家发现，同转基因蔬菜一同生长的杂草，也获得了抗除草剂的特性。

Ⅷ. Theoretical Guidance 翻译理论指导

口译技巧：应对策略

一、预先准备策略。口译工作者在接到口译任务之后，首先应当尽可能多地获取相关信息和材料，以便进行必要和充分的译前准备。俗话说：未雨绸缪，有备无患。口译人员应当事先了解外国代表团的日程安排、会议主要议题、相关技术背景知识等信息，预见工作中可能出现的情况，设想好应对的方案。口译者还需要事先熟悉一些办公设备。

二、临场应对策略。口译现场难免会遇到一些始料未及的情况,俗话说:既来之,则安之。译者不可慌张、怯场,必须灵活运用相应的策略处理出现的问题,保证口译活动正常开展。

请结合口译技巧解析视频,完成下列题目,注意应对策略和技巧的运用。

1. How should we get prepared for interpretation activities in advance?
   A. To prepare for relevant materials.
   B. To get psychologically adjusted and adapted.
   C. To imagine and get ready for possible problems.
   D. To get familiar with the relevant time, location and equipments.

2. To associate with participants in advance can help us get to know about relevant _____, which may make it easier for interpretation during the meeting or negotiation.
   A. thought patterns
   B. ways of expression
   C. particular accents
   D. habitual practices

3. When we meet unfamiliar technical terms or unexpected situations, which of the following should be avoided?
   A. We can ask for expertise help whenever we are in need.
   B. We can overlook unfamiliar expressions and focus on major ones.
   C. We can use transliteration directly.
   D. We can use paraphrase to explain.

Chapter 7　Electronic Technology

电 子 技 术

Ⅰ. Academic Background 学术背景汇报

Directions: *Study the following questions before class and try to search for some relevant information. Then discuss these questions with your group members. Give a brief introduction to the discipline of electronics and present it in class.*

1. What is an electron?
2. Can you make a brief introduction to the sub-disciplines of electronics?
3. What does the study of electronic technology mainly cover?
4. Can you mention some practical applications of electronic communication technology?

Ⅱ. E-C Academic Translation 英汉学术翻译

Directions: *Study the notes in advance. Then read the following passage carefully and translate it into Chinese with the help of the notes supplied. Try to enrich your academic vocabulary and sentence patterns.*

1. artificial intelligence（AI）　人工智能
2. speculation　*n.* 猜测；推测
   speculate *v.* 猜测；推测
3. digital　*adj.* 数字信息系统的；数码的
4. leading　*adj.* 最重要的；一流的；领先的
5. deductive reasoning　演绎推理
6. duplicate　*v.* 复制；复印
7. application　*n.* 应用程序；运用
8. common sense　常识
9. intuition　*n.* 直觉
10. logic inference　逻辑推理
11. attempt to　尝试、试图（做……）
12. reproduce　*v.* 复制；再现
13. imitate　*v.* 模仿；仿效
14. circuitry　*n.* 电路
15. contribute to 有助于；促成
16. agree on　对……意见一致
17. revolutionary　*adj.* 革命的；革新的
18. checkers　*n.* 西洋跳棋
19. ponderous　*adj.* 笨拙的；笨重的
20. consciousness　*n.* 意识；知觉

21. self-awareness   自我认知；自我意识 | 22. mechanized   *adj*. 机械化的

Artificial Intelligence

Serious speculation about whether machines could think started in the 1950s, not too long after the digital computer was invented. A machine designed in 1947 could perform a single move in a chess game, which was proof to some leading computer scientists that machine was capable of deductive reasoning. These scientists believed that "artificial" machines could probably be made to "think" since "natural" machines — humans — could. On the other hand, some other scientists didn't believe that computers would ever duplicate human thinking. Since then, artificial intelligence has been a subject for exploration and debate at major universities.

Expert system, considered one of the most practical applications resulting from AI research so far, began evolving in the late 1970s.

A computer with artificial intelligence will use common sense, judgment, intuition, and make logic inferences — qualities that are now unique to humans. Computer scientists are attempting to build software and computers that can make decisions, learn from their own mistakes, solve problems, and program themselves. The task of developing computers and software to reproduce and imitate the complex circuitry of the brain is an ambitious project.

One problem contributing to the slow progress in artificial intelligence is that people cannot agree on a definition. More accurately, the definition seems to be changing. What was once revolutionary for a computer is now not so extraordinary.

It is pointed out that the first checker and chess games that computers played were considered to be applications of artificial intelligence at that time. Today, there are inexpensive, pocket-sized machines that can play better than those first ponderous devices, but now they are not considered examples of artificial intelligence.

There are other questions: Can a computer possess consciousness, self-awareness, and creativity?

Computers can imitate thought processes such as those necessary to carry out some complex tasks very logically. But do they have intelligence? Some experts have remarked that a computer is still no more than a mechanized idiot servant, i.e., a dumb machine that exhibits a remarkable skill in a limited area.

Ⅲ. C-E Academic Translation 汉英学术翻译

Directions: *Study the notes in advance. Then read the following passage carefully and translate it into English with the help of the notes supplied. Try to enrich your academic vocabulary and sentence patterns.*

1. 机器人程序 bot
2. "斯内普"的机器人程序 SNAPR (Social Network Automated Phishing with Reconnaissance)
3. 社交网络 social network
4. 诱骗;诈骗;欺骗 deceive; cheat; fool; coax
5. 自动化钓鱼系统 automated phishing system
6. 追踪 trace; track
7. 心血来潮;一时兴致;突发奇想 whim
8. 不经意间 inadvertently
9. 间谍软件 spyware
10. 亚历山大大帝 Alexander the Great
11. 推特 Twitter(美国一家社交网络及微博客服务的公司,致力于服务公众对话。Twitter向用户推送的消息被称作"推文")
12. 不知情的,无戒心的 unsuspecting
13. 错误;失策 error; mistake; misstep
14. 引起;诱出 elicit
15. 实力相等;不相上下;与……平分秋色 on par with; equally match
16. 黑客 hacker
17. 编写钓鱼信息 craft phishing messages
18. 可能性;可行性 possibility; feasibility
19. 欺诈(行为/事态) fakery; fraud
20. 愈演愈烈 be more violent; become increasingly fierce; worsen further
21. (类)神经网络 neural network
22. 海量数据 vast amounts of data; massive data
23. 逐步获取,四处搜集 glean
24. 筛查 sift through
25. 红迪网 Reddit (新闻网站)
26. 赋予 endow with; infuse with
27. 类型;种类 breed; type; categary
28. 网民 netizen; cybercitizen
29. 大规模欺诈 massive fraud; mass manipulation
30. 深度伪造技术 deepfakes
31. 色情明星 porn star
32. 完美地 perfectly; seamlessly
33. 更新 update; renew; metabolize
34. 苹果西丽 Apple Siri (苹果智能语音助手)

智 能 诈 骗

这款名为"斯内普"的机器人程序是一个自动化钓鱼系统，能够追踪特定目标的想法，设法诱使他们在不经意间将间谍软件下载到电脑或手机里。"考古学家相信他们在美国首次发现了亚历山大大帝的陵墓。"这就是该钓鱼程序向一位不知情用户发送的推文。

该程序虽然偶尔会出现语法错误，但66%的情况下能够成功诱导用户进行点击操作，与那些手动编写钓鱼信息的黑客不相上下。这个程序实际上并没有携带间谍软件和危险网站，它仅仅是对自动化钓鱼可行性的一个证明。但随着人们对政治性黑客活动、虚假新闻和社交网络阴暗面的担忧日益高涨，这个程序说明了为什么欺诈事态只会愈演愈烈。

该程序搭建起一个类神经网络，这是一个复杂的数学系统，可以通过分析海量数据完成学习任务。例如，类神经网络可以逐步从成千上万张狗的照片中提取模型，从而学会识别狗。它同样可以通过筛查先前的技术支持通话，学会识别口语。类神经网络还可以通过研究推特、红迪网帖子以及之前的网络黑客行为来学习编写钓鱼信息。

当今，从语音识别到翻译，同样的数学技术赋予了机器各种各样类人类的能力。在很多情况下，这种新型的人工智能同样也是在网络上欺骗大量网民的理想手段。大规模欺诈将越来越容易操作。

人工智能不断兴起，发展出深度伪造技术，许多科技观察人士对此表示担忧。深度伪造的图片虽是伪造，看起来却很像是真的。这种技术一开始只是可以将任何人的头移在色情明星肩膀上，到现在演变成能够完美地将任一图片或音频插入到视频中。

研发人员已经开发出可以自我更新并基于不断积累的数据开展学习的系统。网络安全这个威胁便会随之不断加剧。类神经网络可以生成让人信以为真的声音和图像。现在像苹果西丽这样的智能语音助手听起来比几年前更接近真人的声音，原因就在于此。

Ⅳ. Extended Terms and Expressions 词汇拓展训练

Directions: *Fill in the following chart and try to get familiar with these extended terms and expressions.*

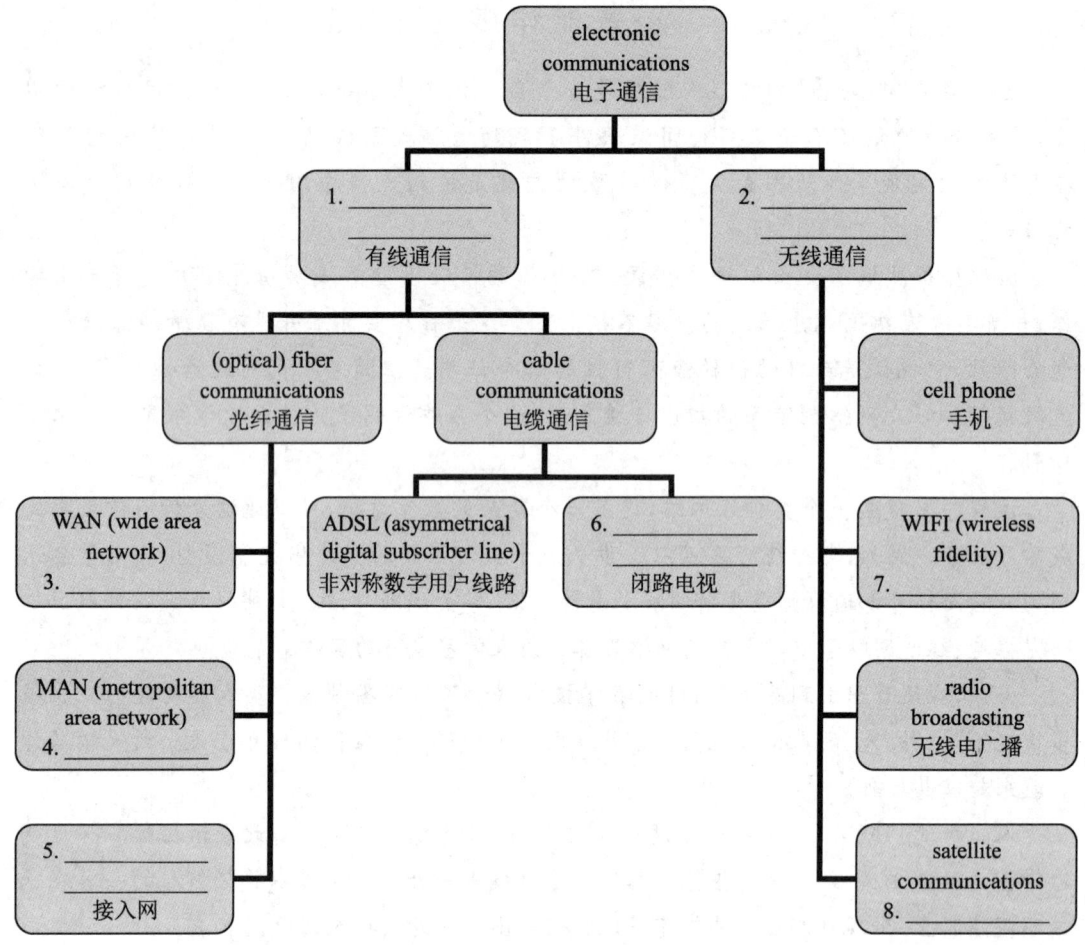

Ⅴ. Sentence Translation 句子翻译训练

Directions: *Each of the following sentences is followed by two versions of translation. Make a comparison between them and decide which one is better. Then discuss with group members and share your viewpoints.*

1. Officials at the Semiconductor Industry Association said the Chinese government has an ambitious $150 billion program to acquire as well as develop new technologies in various kinds of chips.

   A. 据半导体行业协会的官员称，中国政府制定了一个雄心勃勃的计划，打算投入1 500亿美元购买和开发各类芯片的新技术。

   B. 半导体行业协会的一些官员说中国政府有一个投入1 500亿美元购买和开发各类芯片新技术的雄心勃勃的计划。

2. Carmakers fear that the future value of the car will be in the electronic technology and software "brains" linking to the functions, rather than the steel they have been engineering for decades.
   A. 汽车制造商担心,未来汽车的价值将体现在驱动不同功能的电子技术和软件"大脑"上,而不是几十年以来他们设计制造的钢铁躯壳。
   B. 汽车制造者担心汽车的未来价值在于连接功能的电子技术和软件"大脑",而不是他们造了几十年的钢材。

3. By now the secret of radar was unveiled, whose manifold applications extended human eyesight to the longer wavelengths of the electromagnetic spectrum.
   A. 现在,雷达的面纱被揭开了,它的各种应用将人类的视线延伸到电磁光谱中的长波。
   B. 雷达已经揭开了它那神秘的面纱:该技术的各种应用在电磁光谱长波段领域延伸了人类的视线范围。

4. The technical possibilities could well exist, therefore, of nation-wide integrated transmission network of high capacity, controlled by computers, interconnected globally by satellite and submarine cable, providing speedy and reliable communications throughout the world.
   A. 因此,实现高容量、电脑控制、通过卫星和海底电缆实现全球互联并提供遍布全世界的高速可靠通信业务的全国性集成发送网络技术的可能性是完全存在的。
   B. 因此,从技术角度而言,完全可能实现全国性的集成发送网络。这种网络容量大,由计算机控制,并能通过卫星和海底电缆实现全球互联,为世界各地提供高速而可靠的通信服务。

5. Wi-Fi 信号运用强度很弱的无线电波,其波长与家用微波辐射相似,而其强度则比家用微波炉要弱 10 万倍。
   A. Wi-Fi signals use very low intensity radio waves. Whilst similar in wavelength to domestic microwave radiation, the intensity of Wi-Fi radiation is 100,000 times less than that of a domestic microwave oven.
   B. Wi-Fi signal uses very weak radio waves. Its wavelength is nearly the same as family microwave, but its intensity is 100,000 times weaker than a family microwave oven.

6. 3D 和 AR 等现代电子技术的运用让虚拟场景和真实舞台相结合,配上演员们俏皮的舞蹈动作以及一些国宝的展示,让整个节目得以精彩呈现。

A. 3D and AR modern digital technologies combine the virtual scene with the real stage, together with the cute dancing actions of actresses and display of some national treasures, have made the whole show splendid.

B. The use of modern digital technologies such as 3D and AR produces a combination of virtual scene with real stage. Along with the nifty moves of dancers and the demonstration of national treasures, all these make the show brilliant and impressive.

7. 半导体器件在电子设备中能起到各式各样的控制作用。位于上海的半导体制造商中芯国际为打造全国行业领军企业做出了最明显的努力。

A. Semiconductors can play various roles to control. Semiconductor maker SMIC located in Shanghai has made the most obvious efforts to create a leading company among the national industry.

B. Semiconductor devices can perform a variety of control functions in electronic equipments. Shanghai-based semiconductor manufacturer SMIC has represented the most visible attempt at creating a national champion.

8. 为了表示 0~9 的 10 个数字和英文字母表中的 26 个字母，我们需要 0 和 1 的 36 种不同的组合。

A. If we want to illustrate the 10 numbers 0~9 and the 26 English letters, we need 36 different groupings of 0 and 1.

B. To represent the 10 numerals (0, 1, 2, ..., 9) and the 26 letters of the English alphabet would require 36 different combinations of 0 and 1.

Ⅵ. Abstract Translation 摘要翻译训练

Directions: *Go through the list of terminologies and get familiar with these terms. Then try to translate the following abstract into English and learn how to write an abstract in a proper way.*

Terminologies
1. 无线网络 wireless network
2. 通信协议 communication protocol
3. 微波辐射 microwave radiation
4. 网络节点 network node
5. 管理机制 management mechanism
6. 模拟 simulate *v.*; simulation *n.*
7. 链路连接 link connection

Chapter 7 Electronic Technology 电子技术

新型无线网络安全通信协议的设计与模拟

摘要： 无线网络技术是21世纪全球信息技术发展的重要标志之一。无线网络快速发展，使我们更加重视其安全问题。无线网络信息是通过微波辐射传播的，所以只要在无线网络节点覆盖的区域内，所有的工作站都有可能接收到信息，这对信息传播的安全性造成很大的威胁，进而出现各类关于无线网络安全的问题。为了保护无线网络的安全性，要不断完善安全管理机制，以有效防范安全风险，促进无线网络安全健康发展。本课题设计一个简单的无线网络安全通信协议，使其在NS2网络模拟软件中进行模拟，观察其链路连接的过程。通过仿真演示，我们更加了解无线网络安全通信协议在网络中的运行过程，为分析与设计通信协议提供可靠的依据。

关键词： 无线网络技术；无线安全；通信协议

Ⅷ. Academic Debate 学术思辨训练

Directions: *Read the following topic and try to translate the provided viewpoints. Then have a discussion with your group members and find more support for both sides. Hold an English debate in class between two groups. Remember: your arguments can refer to but are not limited to the points provided.*

Debate Topic The advantages for students to use digital products overweigh its disadvantages.

Pros:
1. 电子产品是一种具有联网搜索功能的产品，其快速而强大的检索功能配合网络学习工具可以帮助学生在最短的时间内搜索到自己想要了解的知识。
2. 电子产品是有效的社交工具，电话、微信、QQ……分分秒秒把地球变成一个"小村落"，方便学生之间、师生之间以及家长与孩子之间互通有无。
3. 电子产品的定位功能可以让学生在有需要的时候及时联系老师和家长，紧急情况下还可以报警。
4. 电子产品往往附带游戏功能，只要合理规划，学生可以利用电子游戏适当放松一下，有利于身心健康，也有利于学生以更充沛的精力投入学习。
5. 电子产品可以方便学生的生活，小到水笔、橡皮、黏胶纸，大到课桌、耳机、电脑，只需轻轻一点，所有所需的商品一键搞定。

Cons:

1. 电子产品都有电磁波辐射,学生多用电子产品不利于健康。
2. 电子产品的上网功能太强大,学生由于自控能力相对较弱,经不起诱惑,容易受到网络上"黄赌毒"等不良信息的影响。
3. 电子游戏对学生群体造成了很大的不良影响,不少学生由于沉迷其中,不可自拔,浪费了宝贵的学习时间,玩物丧志,走上歧途。
4. 网络查询功能非常便捷,容易使学生产生依赖感,做作业不喜欢自己动脑筋独立完成,而通过网络搜索快速查找答案,养成了不良的学习习惯。
5. 电子产品的液晶屏存在屏闪。专家指出,学生每次连续使用液晶屏超过20分钟、每天累计使用液晶屏超过1小时,就会对眼睛产生不同程度的伤害。

Ⅷ. Theoretical Guidance 翻译理论指导

口译技巧:记忆训练

我们的记忆分为不同的层面:感觉记忆、短时记忆和长时记忆。每种记忆都有各自的特点和功能。口译活动是一种高度集约化的信息转换和加工过程,需要全方位调动人脑的记忆功能。因此,了解记忆的类别与功能无疑有助于更好地训练我们的记忆,提高大脑处理语言信息的能力,促进口译任务的完成。

记忆容量和提取能力对于完成任何认知任务都十分重要。我们可以通过专门的记忆训练方法提高口译技能。口译过程中,对于信息的储存和记录有两种方式:心记为主,笔记为辅。

请结合口译技巧解析视频,完成下列题目,注意运用记忆训练技巧。

1. Memory relevant to interpretation activities can be classified into _____.
    A. sensory memory   B. short-term memory
    C. long-term memory   D. action memory

2. _____ mainly functions in the form of verbal-audio code with no more than 4 to 9 information modules, which usually lasts around 15 seconds.
    A. Sensory memory   B. Short-term memory
    C. Long-term memory   D. Action memory

3. _____ organizes and stores information permanently by means of words and phrases, as well as video images, sounds, feelings etc.
   A. Sensory memory   B. Short-term memory
   C. Long-term memory   D. Action memory

4. Note-taking is of great help, but _____ of the storing burden is still assumed by our brain.
   A. 30%   B. 50%   C. 70%   D. 90%

5. Which of the following statements is NOT true concerning note-taking?
   A. We should keep a dynamic balance between memorization and note-taking.
   B. We should write down something convenient and easy to handle.
   C. Notes should be easily recognizable and readable.
   D. Notes should be equivocal and one single term should refer to different meanings.

6. Which of the following approaches can be used to improve our memory capacity?
   A. Shadowing.   B. Summarizing.   C. Visualizing.   D. Logical sorting.

7. How can we improve our memory's working capacity concerning interpretation?
   A. To gain precise discourse comprehension.
   B. To conduct practice on STM (short-term memory).
   C. To recite more memory rules and laws.
   D. To expand the storage of LTM (long-term memory).

Chapter 8　Intelligent Manufacturing

智 能 制 造

Ⅰ. Academic Background 学术背景汇报

Directions: *Study the following questions before class and try to search for some relevant information. Then discuss these questions with your group members. Give a brief introduction to the discipline of intelligent manufacturing and present it in class.*

1. What is manufacturing?
2. What is intelligent manufacturing?
3. Can you mention some major techneques involving intelligent manufacturing?
4. Why is intelligent manufacturing important in our life? Give examples.

Ⅱ. E-C Academic Translation 英汉学术翻译

Directions: *Study the notes in advance. Then read the following passage carefully and translate it into Chinese with the help of the notes supplied. Try to enrich your academic vocabulary and sentence patterns.*

1. program　*n*. 程序　*v*. 编程
   re-programmable　*adj*. 可重复编程的
2. multi-functional　*adj*. 多功能的
3. manipulate　*v*. 操作；操纵
   manipulator　*n*. 操作器；操纵者
4. be universally recognized　获得普遍认可；广为接受
5. advent　*n*. 到来；出现
6. industrial revolution　工业革命
7. specialize　*v*. 专门从事；专攻
   specialized　*adj*. 专业化的
8. mechanized　*adj*. 机械化的
9. machinist　*n*. 机械师
10. mechanization　*n*. 机械化
11. drawing　*n*. 图纸
12. specification　*n*. 产品规格；技术参数
13. job order　订单；工作单；作业单
14. process plan　工艺流程；工艺规程；过程计划
15. finished product　成品；制成品
16. interchangeability　*n*. 可互换性；可替代性
17. uniform　*adj*. 一致的；统一的
    uniformity　*n*. 一致性

16. integrate v. 集成；融合
    integration n. 整合；集成；一体化
17. automated adj. 自动化的
    automation n. 自动化
18. component n. 组成部分；成分；部件
19. computer-aided design（CAD） 计算机辅助设计
20. draft n. 草图；起草 v. 起草；绘制
    drafter n. 起草者；绘图员
21. computer numerical control（CNC） 电脑数值控制
22. live up to 符合；达到预期标准
    live up to one's potential 充分发挥潜力
23. computer integrated manufacturing（CIM） 计算机集成制造
24. manual adj. 手工的；体力的
25. straightedge n. 直尺
26. triangle n. 三角形；三角尺
27. scale n. 比例尺
28. diagram n. 图表；图解
29. computer-aided process planning（CAPP） 计算机辅助工艺规划（法）
30. computer-aided manufacturing（CAM） 计算机辅助制造

Revolution of Manufacturing

A robot is a re-programmable, multi-functional manipulator designed to move materials, parts, tools and special devices through a variety of programmed motions to control a variety of different tasks. This definition is universally recognized. The main point is that industrial robots are re-programmable and are capable of different types of path movements.

With the advent of the industrial revolution, manufacturing process became both highly specialized and mechanized. Instead of one person designing, producing and delivering a product, workers and machines performed specialized tasks within each of these broad areas. Communication among these separate entities was achieved using drawings, specifications, job orders, process plans and a variety of other communication aids. To ensure that the finished product matched the planned product, the concept of quality control was introduced.

The positive side of the mechanization stage was that it permitted mass production, interchangeability of parts, different levels of accuracy and uniformity. The disadvantage is that the lack of coordination and integration led to a great deal of waste.

Automation improved the performance and enhanced the capabilities of both people and machines within specialized manufacturing components. For example, computer-aided design（CAD）enhanced the capability of designers and drafters, and computer numerical control（CNC）enhanced the capabilities of machinists and computer-assisted planners. But the improvements brought on by automation were isolated within individual components. Because of this, automation did not always live up to its potential.

Manufacturing seems returning to its original starting point with the coming of the computer age. It began as a totally integrated concept and, with computer integrated manufacturing (CIM), has once again become ONE. However, there are major differences in the manufacturing integration of today and that of the past manual era. First, integration in the manual era was fulfilled by human mind, while in modern manufacturing it is achieved by computer. Second, the process in modern manufacturing setting is specialized and automated.

Another way to view the historical development of CIM is by examining the ways in which some of the individual components of CIM have developed over the years. Such components as design, planning, and production have evolved as processes, and evolvements also take place in the tools and equipments used to accomplish the processes. Design has evolved from a manual process using such tools as straightedge, triangle, pencils, scales, and erasers into an automated process known as CAD; process planning from a manual process using planning tables, diagrams, and charts into an automated process known as computer-aided process planning (CAPP); and production from a manual process involving manually controlled machines into an automated process known as computer-aided manufacturing (CAM).

Ⅲ. C-E Academic Translation 汉英学术翻译

Directions: *Study the notes in advance. Then read the following passage carefully and translate it into English with the help of the notes supplied. Try to enrich your academic vocabulary and sentence patterns.*

1. 柔性自动化技术 flexible automation technology
2. 技术性操作 technical operation
3. 明确的目标,既定目标 set/specific goal
4. 机械工程制造 mechanical engineering manufacture
5. 工业化 industrialization
6. 不可缺少的 indispensable; crucial
7. 数控技术 numerical control technology
8. 高端的 high-end
9. 劳动强度 labor intensity
10. 产品效益 product benefits
11. 发展趋势 developing trend; trend of development
12. 集成自动化技术 integrated automation technology
13. 加强 strengthen; enhance; reinforce
14. 计算机集成系统 computer integrated

system	gain wide recognitions
15. 得到广泛认可 be widely recognized;	

自动化技术

柔性自动化技术是一种基于计算机技术产生的新型自动化技术。这种技术既能够自动进行技术性操作,也能够完成明确的加工目标。当今机械工程制造产业就需要这种能大大提高生产率的技术,从而推动工业化的发展。目前,柔性自动化技术已经成为机械工程制造中不可缺少的一部分,它主要以数控技术为核心,通过有机结合先进的信息科学技术、机械生产技术以及高端计算机设备来发展工业机械制造。

对于工业发展而言,自动化技术在机械工程中的应用意义非凡:(1)可以大幅提高生产效率,增加生产数量,进而大幅降低工人的劳动强度。(2)既能够降低生产成本,又能确保产品质量,从而大幅提高产品效益。通过以上两点可以看出,柔性自动化技术代表着现代机械工业制造行业的发展趋势。

集成自动化技术结合现有的信息技术促进机械工程中各类制造工艺流程的改进和细化,并有效融合生产流程中所有相关的生产信息与技术,进而实现加强集成功能、拓展机械生产的目的。到目前为止,集成自动化技术凭借着上述优势得到了国家机械工程制造的广泛认可。与此同时,随着计算机集成系统的日益改善,集成自动化技术也逐渐涉足其他更多方面。从当今的市场发展来看,这项技术能够从产品研发到生产质控等环节确保收益最大化。

Ⅳ. Extended Terms and Expressions 词汇拓展训练

Directions: *Fill in the following chart and try to get familiar with these extended terms and expressions.*

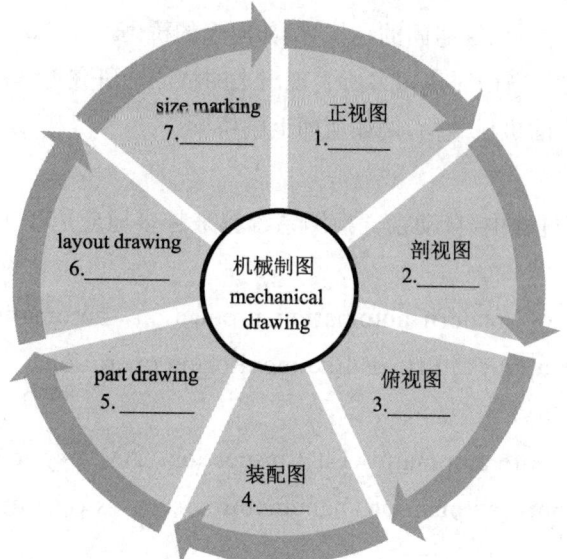

Ⅴ. Sentence Translation 句子翻译训练

Directions: *Each of the following sentences is followed by two versions of translation. Make a comparison between them and decide which one is better. Then discuss with group members and share your viewpoints.*

1. The injection mould should be dimensionally correct.
    A. 注射模具应当尺寸正确。
    B. 注塑模具的尺度必须准确。

2. One property associated with the glassy state is a low volume coefficient of the expansion.
    A. 玻璃态的特征之一是体积膨胀系数较低。
    B. 一个与玻璃质相关的特点即低体积膨胀系数。

3. With the rapid development of modern automation manufacture, it is necessary to develop new inspection ways to ensure the quality of the products.
    A. 随着现代自动化的飞跃发展，新的检测方法十分必要，用来保证产品质量。
    B. 现代化大规模自动生产飞速发展的背景下，为了保障产品质量，有必要更新检测技术。

4. Mechanical properties are the characteristic responses of a material to applied forces. Knowledge of mechanical properties of materials is essential in order to construct a mechanically sound structure such as a bridge on the river.
    A. 机械性质指的是一种材料对作用力的特征性反应。有关材料机械性质的知识很重要，为了能够建造机械性稳固的结构，例如河上的桥。
    B. 力学性质指的是材料面对作用力所表现出来的特征。研究力学性质至关重要，以便人们能够建造可靠的机械结构，例如河面上的桥梁。

5. 在现代自动化生产过程中，自动视觉检测系统越来越多地应用于工况监视、成品检验和质量控制等领域。
    A. In the process of modern automation production, automatic visual test systems more and more applies in fields like monitoring operation, testing production and controlling quality.
    B. Now more and more automatic visual inspection (AVI) systems have been applied in fields of modern automation manufacture, such as operating monitor, product

inspection and quality control.

6. 机械加工不是一种经济的塑形方法,该方法使许多宝贵的原料变成废屑。
   A. Mechanical processing is not an economic way of shape, because it turns many expensive good raw materials into useless wastes.
   B. Machining is not an economical method of producing shape because it has good raw materials converted into hundreds of thousands of scrap chips.

7. 冶金自动化技术和数控技术已经成为支撑钢铁工业可持续发展的核心技术。
   A. Technologies such as metallurgical automation and numerical control have become the core technologies for the sustainable development of iron and steel industry.
   B. Metal automation technology and digital control technology has turned into the key technology for the sustaining development of iron and steel industry.

8. 工业机器人适合在复杂无序的环境中以高精度完成重复劳动,因而广泛应用于工业自动化生产领域。
   A. Industrial robots have been widely applied in automation manufacture fields for their highly repeated precision in complicated and structureless workspace.
   B. Industrial robots are suitable for repeated tasks with high accuracy in complex and disordered environment, so they have been widely used in automatic production.

Ⅶ. Abstract Translation 摘要翻译训练

Directions: *Go through the list of terminologies and get familiar with these terms. Then try to translate the following abstract into English and learn how to write an abstract in a proper way.*

> **Terminologies**
> 1. 智能制造 intelligent manufacturing
> 2. 研究领域 research domain
> 3. 智能多模式终端 intelligent multimode terminal (IMT)
> 4. 框架结构 framework structure
> 5. 智能加工中心 intelligent machining center (IMC)

智能制造的起源、发展与展望

摘要：本文介绍了"智能制造"概念的背景、主要研究领域和目标、人工智能与智能多模式终端(IMT)的关系、智能制造的物质基础及理论基础、智能制造系统的特征及框架结构，并简要介绍了智能加工中心(IMC)、智能制造技术的发展趋势以及智能制造系统研究成果及存在的问题。

关键词：智能制造；智能多模式终端；智能加工中心

Ⅶ. Academic Debate 学术思辨训练

Directions: *Read the following topic and try to translate the provided viewpoints. Then have a discussion with your group members and find more support for both sides. Hold an English debate in class between two groups. Remember：your arguments can refer to but are not limited to the points provided.*

Debate Topic The development of automatic device and intelligent manufacture brings more good than harm to us humans.

Pros：
1. 智能制造无需人工劳作，能够解放劳动力，为我们的生活提供更多的轻松和愉悦。
2. 自动化设备不会感到疲劳，可长时间在危险的工作环境下作业，有助于提高生产效率和生产安全性。
3. 智能制造整条流水线采用自动化管理，生产稳定性强，工艺水平高，产品质量好。
4. 智能制造适合批量生产，有助于降低企业的生产成本。
5. 自动化程序可以代替传统人工手段执行一些手动测试困难或不可能完成的测试，比如针对大量用户的测试，以往不可能同时让足够多的测试员同时测试，现在可以通过自动化测试模拟达到此目的。
6. 自动化使得更多的劳动力释放出来，人类可以有更多的时间和精力从事自己真正喜欢的事情，从事创造性的工作，促进人类文明朝着更高的水平迈进。

Cons：

1. 如果企业全面采纳自动控制与管理，生产过程的技术含量增大，这无疑对企业员工的文化水平和专业知识提出了更高的要求，而且需要开展专门培训，提高了劳动力成本。
2. 自动化设备取代大批的蓝领工人，势必造成失业率上升。大量下岗工人生活无着落，容易造成家庭和社会的不稳定。
3. 在很多需要人脑判断结果的测试过程中无法利用自动工具完成测试，如果企业投入大量研发成本，则代价太大，还不如让技术人员进行人工测试。
4. 机器的智能水平越来越高，有朝一日机器拥有自己的思想和创造力，就有可能反过来控制地球，控制人类世界，我们要尽量避免这可怕的一幕。

Ⅷ. Theoretical Guidance 翻译理论指导

口译技巧：预测听辨

预测，顾名思义就是指在尚未接受到信息，或者尚未接受到完整信息时，根据手头已有的信息以及头脑中储存的信息，经过快速加工匹配，对未知信息进行有依据的猜测。口译人员做出的猜测可能正确，也可能不正确。这就需要利用"听辨"的过程来证实先前正确的猜测，或者更正错误的猜测。

预测和听辨可以从两个层面入手：1) 篇章层面：重点把握中心段、主题句（主题思想和主要脉络）；2) 词汇层面：重点把握名词、动词等实词（关键词）。

请结合口译技巧解析视频，完成下列题目，注意掌握预测听辨技巧。

1. Prediction refers to _____.
   A. a willful guess about the unknown information according to what is stored in one's sensory memory
   B. a reasonable guess about the unknown information based on what is stored in one's short- and long-term memory
   C. a rational guess about the unknown information based on what one hears or reads

2. Prediction should mainly focus on _____.
   A. the main paragraph   B. the topic sentence   C. the whole passage
   D. functional words   E. notional words   F. subordinate clauses

3. Discourse markers mainly include such categories as _____ .

   A. time sequence   B. emphasis   C. explanation

   D. example   E. shifting of topics   F. logical relations

4. Predict the information in the blanks:

China will continue to adhere to the principle of _____ and mutual benefit and develop _____ .

   A. mutual balance; friendly relations with all developed nations

   B. mutual respect; cooperative relations with other nations

   C. mutual assistance; equal relations with developing countries

5. Summarize the key point:

    In fact, desertification is about land degradation: the loss of the land's biological productivity, caused by human-induced factors and climate change. The risks of desertification are substantial and clear. It contributes to food insecurity, famine and poverty, and can give rise to social, economic and political tensions that can cause conflicts, further poverty and land degradation.

   A. The definition, cause, demonstration and hazard of desertification.

   B. The problem of human pollution and its harm to the environment.

   C. The cause of land degradation and the ways to solve it.

Chapter 9 Civil Engineering & Architecture

土 木 建 筑

Ⅰ. Academic Background 学术背景汇报

Directions: *Study the following questions before class and try to search for some relevant information. Then discuss these questions with your group members. Give a brief introduction to the discipline of civil engineering and architecture and present it in class.*

1. Can you briefly introduce the discipline of civil engineering and architecture?
2. What is the primary purpose and practical value of civil engineering and architecture?
3. Which architecture project around the world impresses you most?
4. Can you illustrate the future trend of "green architecture"?

Ⅱ. E-C Academic Translation 英汉学术翻译

Directions: *Study the notes in advance. Then read the following passage carefully and translate it into Chinese with the help of the notes supplied. Try to enrich your academic vocabulary and sentence patterns.*

1. transparent   *adj.* 透明的；清澈的
   semi-transparent   *adj.* 半透明的
2. cement   *n.* 水泥
3. compromise   *v.* 妥协；让步；达不到标准
4. structural integrity   结构完整性
5. concrete   *n.* 混凝土；水泥
6. be akin to   类似于……
7. mesh   *n.* 网状物
8. bond   *v.* 结合；混合
9. resin   *n.* 树脂
10. Italcementi   意大利水泥集团
11. pavilion   *n.* 亭子；场馆
    Italian pavilion   意大利馆
12. World Expo in Shanghai   上海世博会
13. panel   *n.* 水泥板
14. approximately   *adv.* 大约；近似地
15. see-through   *adj.* 透视的
16. modulate   *v.* 调节；调制混合
17. insert   *v.* 插入；嵌入
    insertion   *n.* 插入；嵌入
18. feat   *n.* 壮举
19. optical fiber   光纤
20. fiber optic cable   光纤电缆

21. capture   *v*. 捕获
22. property   *n*. 属性；特性
23. luminous   *adj*. 明亮的；夜光的；透光的
24. take up/meet the challenge   接受挑战
25. at a rate of …   以……的速度
26. patent   *n*. 专利

Transparent Cement

A team of architects in Italy have created "transparent cement" that lets light pour into a room so that the walls look like giant windows. The material, called i.light, has dozens of tiny holes in it which lets light through without compromising the structural integrity. Up close, the 2-3mm gaps make a startling pattern. From certain angles or at a distance, it appears exactly the same as normal concrete. But on a sunny day inside a building made of the cement, the effect is akin to little more than a light mesh on the wall filtering the light coming in.

The cement has been formed by bonding special resins in a new mix created by Italian architects Italcementi. So far they have only used it for one building, the Italian Pavilion at World Expo in Shanghai, and it has already been suggested that it could save electricity that would otherwise be required for daytime lighting.

Italcementi used i.light for around 40 percent of the 18-metre high Expo pavilion, or 3,774 transparent panels and semi-transparent panels made from 189 tonnes of the product. In each transparent panel there are approximately 50 holes, leading to about 20 percent transparency. The semi-transparent panels were around 10 percent see-through and were created by "modulating the insertion of the resins".

Previous attempts at a similar feat had been tried using fiber optic cables through concrete, but Italcementi claims its version is better. The "transparent cement" made from plastic resins is much cheaper than the one made from optical fibers and costs less. Moreover, the ability to "capture" light is greater, since the resins contain a wider visual angle than optical fibers. This characteristic in fact increases the transparency properties of the material and the luminous effects given to buildings. The company took up the challenge to build the pavilion because they wanted to find a "creative, efficient solution". The 3,774 "transparent cement" panels for the Italian Pavilion were made at a rate of around 200 a day. The cement is currently under patent and it is not yet decided if it would be made available worldwide.

Ⅲ. C-E Academic Translation 汉英学术翻译

Directions: *Study the notes in advance. Then read the following passage carefully and* translate it into English with the help of the notes supplied. Try to enrich your academic vocabulary and sentence patterns.

1. 支撑重量 carry/hold up/bear the weight
2. 荷载 load
3. 结构件 structural part
4. 混凝土结构 concrete structure
5. 钢结构 steel structure
6. 砌体结构 masonry structure
7. 钢筋混凝土 reinforced concrete
8. 钢筋 steel reinforcing bar
9. 埋在…… be buried in ...; be embedded in ...
10. 拉应力 tensile stress
11. 抗压强度 compressive strength
12. 充分发挥 bring ... into full play; fully put ... into action
13. 自重 dead weight; dead load
14. 刚度 stiffness
15. 耐久性 durability
16. 养护期 curing period
17. 裂开;开裂 crack
18. 压缩;压力 compression
19. 拉伸 tension
20. 包含;由……组成 be composed of
21. 组建;合成 synthesize
22. 楼板 floor slab
23. 梁 beam
24. 柱 column; pillar
25. 地基 foundation
26. 发挥主导作用 play a leading/dominant role; dominate
27. 立体桁架 three-dimen-sional truss; spatial truss
28. 隔热 heat insulation
29. 脆性材料 brittle material
30. 抗压强度;抗压能力 compressive capacity
31. 抗拉强度;抗拉能力 tensile capacity
32. 可变形能力;形变度;可塑性 deforma-bility
33. 展延性;柔软性 ductility
34. 延性材料 ductile material
35. 地震荷载 earthquake load
36. 超越 exceed
37. 结构抗力 structural resistant capacity
38. 具体说明;明确规定 specify

建 筑 结 构

  结构是建筑物的一部分,支撑着建筑物的重量。结构可能是一幢住宅,也可能是埃及的金字塔,亦或是河上的大坝。建筑物是带有屋顶的结构,而许多土木工程结构设计其实就是建筑物结构设计。建筑物中承受重量和荷载的部分称为结构件。像窗户这种不承重的部分是非结构件。建筑物结构按照建材总类可以分为多种形式,如混凝土结构、钢结构和砌体结构等。

  在钢筋混凝土结构中,钢筋埋入混凝土结构,利用产生的拉应力最大程度地发挥混凝土良好的抗压强度。一般来说,钢筋混凝土结构具有自重大、刚度高、耐久性强、养护期长、易开裂等特点。钢筋混凝土系统包含的各种混凝土构件按照特定的方式组建起来,构成一个整体。这些构件大致可划分为楼板、梁、柱、墙、地基等。

钢结构是一种应用广泛的建筑结构形式,其中钢材发挥主导作用。与混凝土相比,钢材提供了较强的收缩和拉伸能力,并且能够实现更轻便的建筑结构。钢结构使用立体桁架,因此它们能实现比相应的混凝土结构更大的跨度。

砌体的最初应用可以追溯到两千多年前的中国。在钢筋混凝土尚未使用之前,例如石料、砖块以及木材等砌体是主要的建筑材料。即使在现代,由于其较好的隔热性能并易于施工,大多数国家特别是发展中国家依旧使用砌体作为主要的住宅建材。砌体结构以其较低的成本在发展中国家有着很广泛的应用。然而,众所周知,由于砌体材料如砖或砌块是一种脆性材料,其抗压能力强,但其抗拉强度弱,形变度或展延性也都相对较差。由延性材料建造的房屋可以抵御强烈地震,即使遭受严重破坏也不会倒塌;但是一旦地震荷载超过房屋的结构抗力,那些使用脆性材料建造的房屋就会突然倒塌。因此,在可能遭遇强烈地震灾害的区域,必须有严格的条文规定限制建造砌体房屋。

Ⅳ. Extended Terms and Expressions 词汇拓展训练

Directions: *Fill in the following chart and try to get familiar with these extended terms and expressions.*

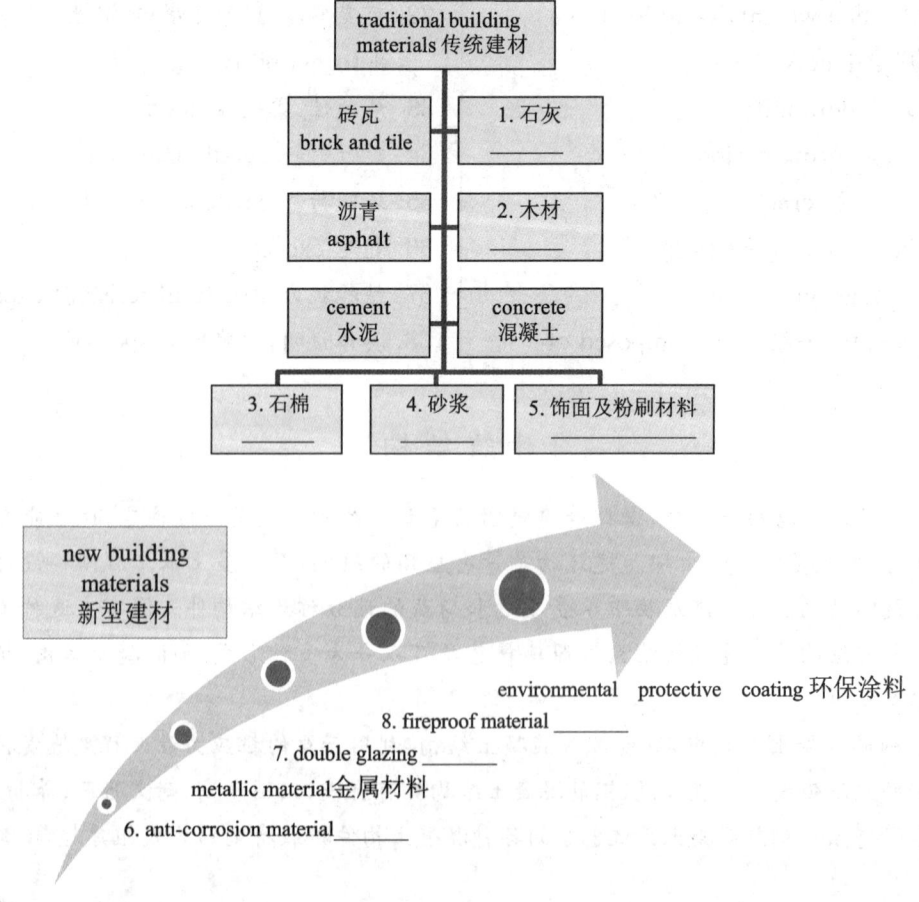

Ⅴ. Sentence Translation 句子翻译训练

Directions: *Each of the following sentences is followed by two versions of translation. Make a comparison between them and decide which one is better. Then discuss with group members and share your viewpoints.*

1. If the anti-seepage measure is not appropriate, the investment would be increased and the original structure of soil mass would be destroyed.
   A. 假如防渗漏措施不合适，投资将会被增加，原有的土壤结构也会被破坏。
   B. 如果防渗漏措施不当，不但会增加投资，土体原有结构还会遭到破坏。

2. The sizes of footing are determined by dividing the loads to be imposed at the base of the footing by the allowable bearing pressure which can be imposed on the soil or rock of the earth.
   A. 基础的尺寸是由加至基础底部的荷载和承受该荷载的土或岩石能够承受的压力来决定的。
   B. 基脚的大小由上部结构传至基脚底部的荷载除以承受该荷载的土或岩石的容许应力来决定。

3. The carrying capacity of the piles may be due to the frictional resistance of the ground against the slides of the piles, in cases where the strength of the ground does not materially increase with depth.
   A. 当土壤强度不随土壤深度的增加而提高，基桩之所以具有承载能力，可能是由于土壤和基桩侧面之间产生摩擦作用。
   B. 基桩的容量可能是由于地面的摩擦阻力对基桩的滑动而产生的，在这种情况下地面的物质强度和深度无关。

4. Where a railway crosses a navigable waterway, and it is impossible to lift the line high enough for vessels to pass underneath without interception, a bridge must be built which is capable of being opened in order to allow the river or canal traffic to pass.
   A. 当铁路经过通航河道，如果无法将铁轨修筑于一定高度以确保下方船只无障碍通行，那么就必须修筑开启式桥梁，以便江河或运河里的船只顺利通行。
   B. 在铁路经过通航河道的地方，若不可能把线路升到足够的高度使船舶通过下面而没有被阻拦，那么桥梁必须被修建，并能够随时被打开，方便水路交通运输。

5. "现场"指工程师设计的永久工程或临时工程所需的土地和其他场所,包括地面、地下、工程范围之内或途经的部分。

   A. "Location" means the permanent works or temporary works designed by an engineer around the land and other places, including floor, underground, places within or towards the project.

   B. "Site" refers to the land and other places on, under, in or through which the permanent works or temporary works designed by the engineer are to be executed.

6. 板式基础或筏式基础通常是一些面积、厚度及配筋量都很大的钢筋混凝土板块,其作用是将柱子或墙上的荷载传到下卧土层或岩层中。

   A. Mat or raft foundations are large, thick, and usually heavily reinforced concrete mats which transfer loads from a number of columns or walls to the underlying soil or rock.

   B. Mat foundation or raft foundation is the concrete plates with large area, deep depth and thick steel bars. Their role is to send the loads of pillars or walls to the soil or rock under them.

7. 目前已经建成了主跨超过 3 000 英尺的悬桥,而整个桥面的重量都是由从两岸的桥塔悬挂下来的钢缆(一般两到四根)自上而下支撑的。

   A. At present, suspension bridges with over 3,000 feet main spans have been built, and the whole weight of the bridge floor is supported by wires (two to four in general) hanging down from the bridge towers on both sides of the river.

   B. There are in existence suspension bridges with main spans of more than 3,000 feet and the entire weight of the deck being supported from above by cables (usually two or four in number) suspended between two towers at either side of the river.

8. 在漫长的发展历程中,出色的建筑技巧和艺术设计融为一体,使得独特的中国建筑成为全世界最杰出的三大建筑体系之一。

   A. During its long development, outstanding architecture skills combine with artistic designs, and make the special Chinese architecture one of the three greatest architecture systems in the world.

   B. A gradual process of development nurtures the integration of superior architectural techniques and artistic designs, making the unique Chinese architecture one of the world's three greatest architectural systems.

Ⅵ. Abstract Translation 摘要翻译训练

Directions: *Go through the list of terminologies and get familiar with these terms. Then try to translate the following abstract into English and learn how to write an abstract in a proper way.*

> **Terminologies**
> 1. 水力工程学 hydraulic engineering 2. 应力状态 stress state
> 3. 渗透系数 permeability coefficient 4. 泥质粉砂岩 clayey siltstone
> 5. 弹性形变 elastic deformation
> 6. 塑性变形；塑性应变 plastic deformation
> 7. 蠕变 creep deformation   8. 应力应变曲线 stress-strain curve
> 9. 层面；层理面 bedding plane   10. 孔隙（率/度）porosity

软岩渗透性、应变及层理关系的试验研究

摘要：在土木、水利及核废料处置工程中，应力状态对岩石渗透性的影响已逐渐成为一个无法回避的问题。本文通过瞬态压力脉冲法，测试泥质粉砂岩和褐红色泥岩等两种典型软岩全应力—应变过程中的渗透系数。试验结果表明：①泥质粉砂岩的渗透系数在弹性阶段逐渐减小，在随后的塑性变形及破坏阶段逐渐增大；垂直于层理方向上的渗透系数大于平行于层理方向上的渗透系数。②褐红色泥岩的渗透系数在塑性变形阶段逐渐减小，而在蠕变阶段基本不变；垂直于层理方向上的渗透系数和平行于层理方向上的渗透系数无明显差异。结合试验中同时得到的应力应变曲线，认为在弹性变形阶段，泥质粉砂岩的渗透系数主要受孔隙和微裂隙控制，而在塑性变形和破坏阶段，渗透系数主要受裂隙影响。褐红色泥岩的渗透系数在整个应变过程中同时受孔隙和微裂隙的影响，两者的作用没有明显差别。

关键词：岩石力学；软岩；全应力应变曲线；渗透系数；层理面；试验研究

Ⅶ. Academic Debate 学术思辨训练

Directions: *Read the following topic and try to translate the provided viewpoints. Then have a discussion with your group members and find more support for both sides. Hold an English debate in class between two groups. Remember: your arguments can refer to but are not limited to the points provided.*

Debate Topic It is beneficial to carry out unified housing planning and build community buildings in rural areas.

Pros:

1. 农村统一规划，建成小区式建筑，农民集中居住，有助于改善农村的公共卫生环境，提高农民生活水平。
2. 农村小区化不仅改善居住条件，而且随之而来的教育资源、医疗设施和购物环境等也会相继好转。例如小区附近开办学校、开设医院、经营超市等都是常见的配套服务。
3. 集中居住的一大优势是便于人员管理，例如新冠疫情之类的传染病大流行期，农村小区化就显现出极大优势，与分散居住相比，更容易开展检疫、盘查、隔离等工作。
4. 由于农村青壮年人口流失，近年来出现了严重的"空心村"现象，不少家庭只有老人和留守儿童住在老家，社区化管理有助于解决老龄化问题和儿童成长中所遇到的心理问题。

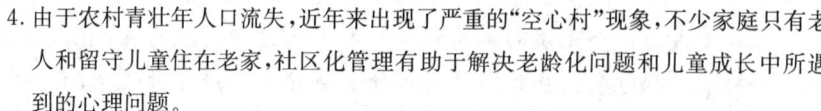

Cons:

1. 农村地区，农田分布比较广泛和分散，集中居住有可能造成居住地远离生产区域，从而导致农民"通勤"忙农务，费时费力。
2. 农村小区化建设实现了农民上楼居住，与原来分散居住相比实际居住面积有所缩减，这是一个不争的事实，很多农用器具没有地方存放，而且上下楼搬运也很不方便。
3. 对于农村老人而言，尤其是那些儿女进城打工不在身边、自己腿脚又不大灵便的老人，搬进高楼之后，如果不是居住一楼又没有电梯的话，势必给从事农活带来诸多不便。
4. 由于利益驱使，农村小区化进程会吸引开发商不断开发新的楼盘，推动农村城市化发展，这些商业行为势必导致更多的农田被占，耕地减少，不利于农业发展和粮食供给。

Ⅷ. Theoretical Guidance 翻译理论指导

口译技巧：速记技巧

速记是口译过程中一个非常实用的技巧，能够有效缓解记忆压力，协助口译人员出色完成口译任务。这里，我们需要解决两个问题：

1. 速记记什么？①记语法角度的主要信息，主谓宾结构的中心词；②记新信息，忽略已知信息；③记密度大和难度高的信息，如数字、专有名词、专业术语等。

2. 速记怎么记？①少写多划；②少字多意；③少线多指；④少横多竖；⑤快速书写；⑥明确结束。

请结合口译技巧解析视频，完成下列题目，注意掌握速记技巧。

1. Which of the following calls for special attention when it comes to note-taking?
    A. SVO (main grammatical structure).
    B. New information.
    C. Numbers.
    D. Technical terms.

2. We can use lines in note-taking to _____.
    A. demonstrate a certain changing trend
    B. display interpersonal relations
    C. illustrate cause-effect relations
    D. show time sequence

3. Which of the following is a correct way of taking notes?
    A. To write quickly and readably.
    B. To write in a top-down manner.
    C. To write from left to right.
    D. To use simple geometric figures.
    E. To use complete sentences.
    F. To use abbreviations.
    G. To scraw quickly and carelessly.
    H. To make a clear stop for a relatively complete period.
    I. To use mathematical symbols.

4. Which of the following abbreviations has been correctly translated?

   A. FOB 到岸价
   B. CFR 成本加运费价
   C. CIF 离岸价
   D. UNESCO 联合国教科文组织
   E. y 年；m 月；w 周；d 日
   F. h 小时；m 分钟；s 秒
   G. IMF 国际劳工组织
   H. ILO 国际货币基金组织
   I. UNCF 联合国儿童基金会
   J. IOC 国际货币组织
   K. MOFCOM 外交部
   L. info 信息
   M. gym 体育馆
   N. ed 教育
   O. grad 毕业生

5. Which of the following statements is true as far as note-taking is concerned?

   A. Exclamation marks or underlines can be used to show emphasis.
   B. Question marks can be used to show doubt.
   C. Arrows can be used to show correctness and acceptance.
   D. "×" can be used to show affirmation，while "√" can be used to show denial.
   E. Colons can be used to show a certain kind of relation.

Chapter 10　Perfume & Aroma

香 精 香 料

Ⅰ. Academic Background 学术背景汇报

Directions: *Study the following questions before class and try to search for some relevant information. Then discuss these questions with your group members. Give a brief introduction to the discipline of perfume and aroma and present it in class.*

1. Why do people like perfume? Can you mention any world-famous perfume brands?
2. What is the development history of perfume and aroma?
3. What are the differences between synthetic and natural fragrances?
4. Can you introduce the technology for scent extraction and purification?

Ⅱ. E-C Academic Translation 英汉学术翻译

Directions: *Study the notes in advance. Then read the following passage carefully and translate it into Chinese with the help of the notes supplied. Try to enrich your academic vocabulary and sentence patterns.*

1. perfume　*n*. 香水
   perfumery　*n*. 香水制造厂；香水商店；香水制造
2. in terms of 依据；按照；从……方面
3. flagship　*n*. 旗舰；王牌
4. luxury-goods　*n*. 奢侈品
5. cosmetics　*n*. 化妆品
6. at an altitude of 海拔为……
7. horticulture　*n*. 园艺；园艺学
8. notably　*adv*. 特别；非常；尤其；显著地
9. jasmine　*n*. 茉莉花
10. aroma　*n*. 香味；芳香；香气；香料
11. fragrance　*n*. 香气；香水；香料
12. lavender　*n*. 薰衣草；淡紫色
13. myrtle　*n*. 桃金娘
14. mimosa　*n*. 含羞草
15. move with the times 与时俱进
16. synthetic　*adj*. 人造的；(人工)合成的
17. extract　*n*. 提取物　*v*. 提取；提炼
18. concentrate　*n*. 浓缩物　*v*. (使)浓缩
19. maceration　*n*. 离析；[化]浸软；浸渍（作用）
20. soak　*v./n*. 浸泡；浸湿
21. distill　*v*. 蒸馏；提取

089

distillation   n. 蒸馏法；蒸馏
22. essential oil   n. 精油
23. blend   v. 混合；融合   n. 混合；混合物
24. cheaper end 低端
25. scent   n. 香味；香水   v. 嗅出；闻到
26. top-of-the-range   （同类产品中）最昂贵的；顶级的
27. lucrative   adj. 赚大钱的；获利多的
28. purveyor   n. 提供者；供应商

French Perfumes

When it comes to the art of perfumes, no country ranks more highly than France. Many of the greatest names in the perfume industry, Chanel, Christian Dior or Estée Lauder are French, and in terms of international perfume sales, France certainly takes the lead, with 30% of the global market. France's flagship company LVMH is the greatest luxury-goods company in the world, and French perfumes and cosmetics are among its most important brands.

Today, while the big names of the perfume industry are based in Paris, and "perfumes from Paris" are particularly appreciated, the real heart of the French perfume industry is actually the small town of Grasse, northwest of Nice. Some 20 km from the coast and at an altitude of 350 metres, Grasse enjoys a mild Mediterranean climate that is particularly suited to horticulture, notably the production of jasmine, one of the most important natural aromas used by the perfume industry. Of course, Grasse is also famous for its production of many other natural fragrances, including lavender, myrtle, roses and mimosa.

The perfume industry in Grasse involves some sixty different companies, and employs almost 3,500 people. Even though Grasse has had to move with the times and now produces synthetic as well as natural fragrances, it is the latter for which it remains justly famous. The great art of perfumery is extracting the fragrances of flowers and concentrating them in forms from which they can be transformed into the perfumes that are eventually sold in little bottles at very high prices. The historic methods of extracting fragrances from flowers are either by maceration (soaking the flowers in a liquid that will absorb their fragrances) or by distillation. The resulting concentrates are known as "essential oils", and it is from these that perfumes are blended and made.

In recent years, particularly at the cheaper end of the scale, the natural fragrances extracted from flowers and other plants have been largely replaced by chemically produced scents, which can be mass-produced anywhere in the world. But in the production of top-of-the-range high quality perfumes made from natural extracts of plants, nothing can replace the acquired skills of France's master perfume producers. The secrets and techniques have been passed down from generation to generation under the Mediterranean sun in the area of Grasse, the essence of which just cannot be replicated or copied. In spite of the lucrative nature of the French perfume industry, other countries have so far found it impossible to challenge France's reputation as purveyor of fine perfumes to the world.

Ⅲ. C-E Academic Translation 汉英学术翻译

Directions: *Study the notes in advance. Then read the following passage carefully and translate it into English with the help of the notes supplied. Try to enrich your academic vocabulary and sentence patterns.*

1. 香料 fragrance; perfume; spice; scent
2. 文化习俗 cultural customs
3. 密不可分的 be closely connected/related to
4. 在古代 in ancient times; in antiquity
5. 热衷于 be keen on; be absorbed in; be fascinated by
6. 制香艺术 the art of perfumery
7. 追溯到 be traced back to; date back to; go back to; date from
8. 美索不达米亚 Mesopotamia
9. （尤指难闻的）气味；臭味 odor
10. 滋润的，保湿的 moisturizing
11. 药膏；膏油 ointment
12. 过滤 filter
13. 揉进 rub into
14. "可菲"神香 Kyphi
15. 精炼 refine
16. 高纯度 high purity
17. 祭司 priest
18. 法老 pharaoh
19. 普及的；盛行的；普遍存在的 common; prevalent
20. 香精 perfume essence
21. 发掘 unearth; excavate
22. 木乃伊 mummy
23. 防腐性 corrosion resistance
24. 永存的 everlasting; enduring; eternal; immortal
25. 神化 deify
26. 祝福 blessing
27. 宗教仪式 religious rite; religious ritual; religious ceremony
28. 工艺方法 technological process; craft method
29. 中世纪早期 the early Middle Ages
30. 大规模的 large-scale
31. 溶解 dissolve
32. 保存 preserve; conserve

香料的发展

香料的使用由来已久。香料的发展与国家的文化习俗和生活习惯密不可分,因而在不同国家的发展历程也不尽相同。在古代,古希腊人和古罗马人热衷于使用香料。事实上,制香艺术可以一直追溯到西方文明在美索不达米亚地区的起源时期。当时,人们使用香料和香水来掩盖身体的异味,进而让人散发迷人的香味儿。这是沐浴时刻非常重要的一项日常活动。

古埃及人使用香料的历史可上溯到公元前3500年左右,远早于其他任何文明。古埃及人学会了制造香水和滋润药膏的方法:用油浸泡香料植物,再用布把这种液体过滤一下,或者把花瓣揉进脂肪里面,吸收和保存它们的香味。人类最早的香水就是埃及人发明的"可菲"神香,由祭司和法老独家调制而成,但是由于当时人们并未掌握精炼高纯度酒精的方法,所以确切地应该称其为香油。公元前1500年,香水在古埃及开始普及。例如,人们在沐浴过程中或沐浴之后都会普遍使用香精和油膏。现代发掘的古代墓葬品已证实,古人将香水存放在造型优美的容器里。当时,埃及人不涂香水出入于公共场所甚至是违法的。人们死后,埃及人用香料裹尸,制成木乃伊。他们相信香料的防腐性可以帮助灵魂永存。

古希腊把香水神化了,认为香水是众神的发明,闻到香味意味着众神降临赐祝福。妇女们在宗教仪式上必须使用香水。在古希腊,制作香水的妇女借鉴了古埃及人的工艺方法,并且在此基础上有所改进。

中世纪早期,阿拉伯人发明了大规模的植物蒸馏法,由此推动了香水发展史的一大进步。12世纪,阿拉伯人又发现将香精以酒精溶解,便可缓缓释放出香味,部分浓缩精华也因酒精得到了更好的保存。

Ⅳ. Extended Terms and Expressions 词汇拓展训练

Directions: *Fill in the following table and try to get familiar with these extended terms and expressions.*

French Terms	English Terms	Chinese Terms	Flavor Content	Alcohol content	Duration of Fragrance
EDF (EAU DE FRAI-CHEUR)	1. _____	清淡香水;须后水	2. _____	<80%	1 hour
EDC (Eau de Cologne)	body spray	3. _____	2%~5%	60%~70%	4. _____
EDT (Eau de Toilette)	5. _____	淡香水	5%~10%	6. _____	3~4 hours
EDP (Eau de Parfum)	perfume	7. _____	7%~15%	80%~85%	8. _____
P (Parfum)	9. _____	浓香精;纯香水	10. _____	70%~85%	5~7 hours

Ⅴ. Sentence Translation 句子翻译训练

Directions: *Each of the following sentences is followed by two versions of translation. Make a comparison between them and decide which one is better. Then discuss with group members and share your viewpoints.*

1. Chanel is about to launch a softer version of this scent for a new generation, suitable for day-time wear and a younger crowd.
    A. 香奈儿即将为年轻一代推出这款柔和版香水,适用于白天涂抹,更适合低龄客户群。
    B. 香奈儿打算推出一款更柔和的香水给新生一代,适合白天时间涂抹和更年轻的人群。

2. The men's fragrance market has continued to grow despite the global financial crisis, albeit at a slower pace.
    A. 男士香水市场继续增长,尽管面临全球金融危机,但却呈现出更加缓慢的速度。
    B. 即使在全球金融危机背景下,男士香水市场消费仍持续走高,尽管增长速度有所减缓。

3. Originating in Spain, Angelica Root was one of the few spices that were actually exported from Europe to the Orient.
    A. 原产于西班牙,当归是数量较少的从欧洲出口到东方的香料之一。
    B. 从欧洲出口到东方的香料为数不多,当归就是其中的一种,原产于西班牙。

4. In Romean Times, the rich Romans were indulging in luxury: spices and paint were used on the floors and walls, perfume was sprayed on the triumphant flag, and rose petals were spread everywhere.
    A. 古罗马时期,富裕的罗马人沉迷奢华:居然用香料涂饰地板和墙壁,凯旋的军旗上也喷洒了香水,到处都撒满了玫瑰花瓣。
    B. 在罗马时代,富裕的罗马人尽情享乐:香料和油漆被用于地板和墙壁,凯旋的军旗被喷洒香水,玫瑰花瓣被四处抛撒。

5. 在波斯古国,香水是身份和地位的象征,因此皇宫里最香的非皇帝莫属。为了提炼玫瑰精油,人们在大片大片的土地上栽种玫瑰。
    A. In the old anntry of Persia, perfume is a symbol of identity and status, so the emperor was the most fragrant in the whole palace. In order to get rose oil, many lands were planted roses.

B. Perfume is a symbol of identity and status in ancient Persia, so the most fragrant in the palace was nothing but the emperor. A large area of land was used to plant roses for the purpose of refining rose oil.

6. 广藿香精油具有促进细胞再生的特点,可用于治疗多种皮肤保养问题,在现代香水制造业中也得到了广泛的应用。

   A. Patchouli essential oil can be good for a variety of skincare treatments with its cell-regeneration properties. It has also been extensively used in modern perfumery.

   B. Patchouli essential oil has the feature of promoting cells to reproduce, can be used for various skincare problems, and is widely used for perfume manufacturing.

7. 雪松油可用于制药和香料,因此备受青睐。为改进香气质量,主张以水蒸气蒸馏技术取代水上蒸馏法。

   A. Cedar wood oil can be used in drugs and perfumes, so it is very popular. In order to improve the odour quality, we support to use steam distillation technology instead of water distillation.

   B. Cedar wood oil is highly prized for its use in medicine and perfumery. Steam distillation is technically recommended to replace water distillation so as to improve its aroma quality.

8. 人们还发现了一些更具魅力的香料新品种,比如麝香。人们甚至将它混入泥浆来建造巴格达宫殿,使之散发出浓烈而持久的香味。

   A. People also found some charming new spices, for example musk. People even mixed it with mud to build the Baghdad palace, letting it send off a strong and forever smell.

   B. Some new and more attractive spices, such as musk, were also discovered, which was even mixed into mud to build the palace in Baghdad, making it emit a strong and lasting fragrance.

Ⅵ. Abstract Translation 摘要翻译训练

Directions: *Go through the list of terminologies and get familiar with these terms. Then try to translate the following abstract into English and learn how to write an abstract in a proper way.*

Terminologies

1. 香兰素 vanillin
2. 阿魏酸 ferulic acid
3. 基底；底物 substrate
4. 微生物转化 microbio-transformation
5. 氮源 nitrogen source
6. 补料 feeding
7. 生物催化剂 biocatalyst
8. 发酵罐 fermentator

微生物转化制备香兰素新工艺

摘要：香兰素是应用最为广泛的香料之一。本研究以阿魏酸为底物，通过微生物转化制备香兰素，考查不同氮源、补料数量和补料方式等生物催化剂因素对阿魏酸转化率的影响。50升发酵罐实验条件下的数据显示，香兰素的最终浓度为15克/升，发酵单位达到国际先进水平。

关键词：微生物转化；香兰素；阿魏酸

Ⅶ. Academic Debate 学术思辨训练

Directions: *Read the following topic and try to translate the provided viewpoints. Then have a discussion with your group members and find more support for both sides. Hold an English debate in class between two groups. Remember: your arguments can refer to but are not limited to the points provided.*

Debate Topic There is great significance in purpusing those international brands of luxurious perfumes.

Pros:
1. 最初人们发明香水，是因为当时条件所限，人们无法经常沐浴，喷洒香水可以掩盖身体的异味；现如今，喷香水还不如勤洗澡、勤洗头、勤更衣，搞好个人卫生。
2. 香水行业长期暴利，尤其是名牌香水，很小的一瓶标价不菲。普通大众为了追求时尚，花费高额金钱购买香水确实属于一种奢侈行为，铺张浪费不值得提倡。
3. 人工合成的香料与天然香料成分相近，功能相同，因此没有多大意义购买天然香料制作而成的"天价香水"。
4. 每个人的气味是一个人独特个性的延伸，代表着与众不同的你和我。大家都喷洒香水，千篇一律，反而失去了个性。

Cons：

1. 香水代表一个人的气质。年龄不同，职业不同，爱好不同，心情不同，选择的香水各不相同。香水会无声无息地告诉周围的人：我每天都在成长，每天都在迎接全新的自我。
2. 香水代表一个人的个性。除了可以选择不同款香型，即使同款香水，由于每个人的体味、体温以及血液循环速度不同，喷洒之后的效果也是千人千面。
3. 在一些重要场合，高端品牌的香水可以提升一个人的品味和相互的认同感，使得我们更加得体地表现自己，达到事半功倍的效果。
4. 高端天然香料制成的香水能给自己和周围的人带来轻松愉悦之感，有些香型，比如玫瑰、茉莉等，有安神、减压、舒缓紧张情绪的作用，长期喷洒有利于身心健康。

Ⅷ. Theoretical Guidance 翻译理论指导

口译技巧：处理数字

在口译工作中，数字几乎无处不在。准确迅速地完成数字口译是口译人员必须掌握的基本功之一。有效地处理数字，一直以来既是口译实践过程中的一大重点，又是一大难点。稍有不慎，就容易出错。研究显示：英译汉数字口译的难点在于"精准识记"；而汉译英数字口译的难点在于"快速表达"。建议大家使用"符号代替单位"的技巧记录数字，使用"找准数位对应"的技巧转换数字。希望大家多加练习，掌握好各类数字的英汉互译，提高口译实践能力。

请结合口译技巧解析视频，完成下列题目，注意掌握处理数字的技巧。

1. Which of the following matching is correct?

    A. ten thousand 万　　　　　　B. million 十万

    C. ten million 千万　　　　　　D. one hundred thousand 百万

    E. one hundred million 亿　　　F. trillion 万亿

2. Which of the following note-taking concerning the big number "**six hundred and ninety-two thousand nine hundred and thirteen**" is more convenient?

    A. 692th　913　　　　　　　　B. 6h　92th　9h　13

3. Which of the following note-taking concerning the big number "**nine hundred and thirty-eight million seven hundred and fifty-seven thousand four hundred and sixty-three**" is more convenient?

A. 9h　38m　7h　57th　4h　63　　　B. 938,757,463

4. How should we translate the big number **"5,236,489,371"** into Chinese?
    A. 5,|236,|489,|371　　五亿两百三十六万四百八十九千零三百七十一
    B. 52|36,48|9,371　　五十二亿三千六百四十八万九千三百七十一

附录 1

全国大学英语四级考试
翻译题型指南及真题演练

全国大学英语四级考试是大学阶段的重要考试之一,而翻译又是四级考试中一个非常关键的题型。2013年,四级考试的翻译题型经历了一场改革,从先前的汉译英句子翻译调整为汉译英段落翻译。这无疑对考生提出了更高的要求:不仅需要考虑词汇、短语在特定语境中的含义以及句子内部各个成分之间的重组,还需要分析句子之间的逻辑关系,处理好句子与句子的相互衔接。翻译内容涉及文化、历史、社会、教育、地理、旅游、经济、科技等各个领域。考生尤其需要关注中国传统文化和历史,以及新时代中国欣欣向荣的发展,这将成为翻译考查的重点。下面为广大考生整理考试简介、评分标准、考试技巧、真题演练等相关信息,请大家认真观看解析视频,一起了解探究,不断提高。

全国大学英语四级考试翻译题型简介

考题篇幅	140—160个汉字
答题时间	30分钟
分值占比	15%(满分15分)
考查要求	1) 准确:用词准确,句子表达含义准确,避免漏译、错译; 2) 通顺:译文符合英语的语法结构和语用习惯,逻辑通顺
注意事项	1) 合理分配时间:用1分钟通读原文,把握语篇所属领域,调动相关中英词汇及该领域的背景知识;预留3分钟用于最后的检查; 2) 遇到个别生僻词,不要停留过长的时间,尽量根据上下文的逻辑关系和词性判断该词在句子中的成分,推测词汇的大致含义; 3) 遇到结构复杂、篇幅较长的句子,尽量避免机械地直译,必须在理解原文的基础上重新组织译文语序,灵活运用学过的句式转换、词性转换等翻译技巧,提高译文质量; 4) 翻译完成后,通读译文,比对原文,确保译文忠实于原文,对表达不地道的译文进行修改和润色,避免"翻译腔",提高译文可读性

全国大学英语四级考试翻译题型评分标准

档次	分值	译文描述
优秀	13—15分	译文准确表达了原文的意思。用词贴切,行文流畅,基本上无语言错误,仅有个别小错
良好	10—12分	译文基本上表达了原文的意思。结构较清晰,文字通顺、连贯,无重大语言错误
及格	7—9分	译文勉强表达了原文的意思。译文勉强连贯,用词欠准确,语言错误相当多,其中有些是严重语言错误

(续表)

档次	分值	译文描述
不及格	4—6分	译文仅表达了一小部分原文的意思。译文连贯性差,用词不准确,有相当多的严重语言错误
	1—3分	译文支离破碎。除个别词语或句子,绝大部分文字没有表达原文意思
	0分	未作答,或只有几个孤立的词,或译文与原文毫不相关

真 题 演 练

1. 中国结最初是由手工艺人发明的。经过数百年不断的改造,已经成为一种优雅多彩的艺术和工艺。在古代,人们用它来记录事件,但现在主要用于装饰的目的。"结"在中文里意味着爱情、婚姻和团聚。中国结常常作为礼物交换或用作饰品祈求好运和避邪。这种形式的手工艺代代相传,现在已经在中国和世界各地越来越受欢迎。(145字)

2. 中国汉族人的全名由姓和名组成。中文姓名的特点是,姓总是在前,名跟在其后。千百年来,父姓一直世代相传。然而,如今孩子跟母亲姓并不罕见。一般来说,名有一个或两个汉字,通常承载父母对孩子的愿望。从孩子的名字可以推断出父母希望孩子成为什么样的人,或者期望他们过什么样的生活。父母非常重视给孩子取名,因为名字往往会伴随孩子一生。(160字)

3. 中国的家庭观念与其文化传统有关。和睦的大家庭曾非常令人羡慕。过去四代同堂并不少见。由于这个传统,许多年轻人婚后继续与父母同住。如今这一传统正在发生变化。随着住房条件的改善,越来越多年轻夫妇选择与父母分开住。但他们之间的联系仍然很密切。许多老年人仍然帮着照看孙辈。年轻夫妇也常抽时间探望父母,特别是在春节和中秋节等重要节日。(160字)

4. 中国家庭十分重视孩子的教育。许多父母认为应该努力工作,确保孩子接受良好的教育。他们不仅非常情愿为孩子的教育投资,而且花很多时间督促孩子学习。多数家长希望孩子能上名牌大学。由于改革开放,越来越多的家长能送孩子到国外学习或参与国际交流项目,以拓宽其视野。通过这些努力,他们期望孩子健康成长,为国家的发展和繁荣作出贡献。(157字)

5. 剪纸是中国民间艺术的一种独特形式,至今已有2 000多年的历史。剪纸很可能源于汉代,继纸张发明之后。从此,它在中国的许多地方得到了普及。剪纸用的材料和工具很简单:纸和剪刀。剪纸作品通常是用红纸做成的,因为红色在中国传统文化中与幸福相联。因此,在婚礼、春节等喜庆场合,红颜色的剪纸是门窗装饰的首选。(141字)

6. 过去几年里,移动支付市场在中国蓬勃发展。随着移动互联网的出现,手机购物逐渐成为一种趋势。18到30岁的年轻人构成了移动支付市场的最大群体。由于现在用手机付款很容易,许多消费者在购物时宁愿用手机付款而不愿用现金或信用卡。为了鼓励人们多消费,许多商店给使用移动支付的顾客打折。专家预测,中国移动支付市场未来仍有很大发展潜力。(158字)

7. 灯笼起源于东汉,最初主要用于照明。在唐代,人们用红灯笼来庆祝安定的生活。从那时起,灯笼在中国的许多地方流行起来。灯笼通常用色彩鲜艳的薄纸制作,形状和尺寸各异。在中国传统文化中,红灯笼象征生活美满和生意兴隆,通常在春节、元宵节和国庆等节日期间悬挂。如今,世界上许多其他地方也能看到红灯笼。(143字)

8. 由于通信网络的快速发展,中国智能手机用户数量近年来以惊人速度增长。这极大地改变了许多人的阅读方式。他们现在经常在智能手机上看新闻和文章,而不买传统报刊。大量移动应用程序的开发使人们能用手机读小说和其他形式的文学作品。因此,纸质书籍的销售受到了影响。但调查显示,尽管智能手机阅读市场稳步增长,超半数成年人仍喜欢读纸质书。(159字)

9. 华山位于华阴市,距西安120公里。华山是秦岭的一部分,秦岭不仅分隔陕南与陕北,也分隔华南与华北。与从前人们常去朝拜的泰山不同,华山过去很少有人光临,因为上山的道路极其危险。然而,希望长寿的人却经常上山,因为山上生长着许多药草,特别是一些稀有的药草。自上世纪90年代安装缆车以来,华山的参观人数大大增加。(148字)

10. 在中国文化中,红色通常象征着好运、长寿和幸福,在春节和其他喜庆场合,红色到处可见。人们把现金作为礼物送给家人或亲密朋友时,通常放在红信封里。红色在中国流行的另一个原因是人们把它与中国革命和中国共产党相联系。然而,红色并不总是代表好运与快乐。因为从前死者的名字常用红色书写。因此,通常认为用红墨水写中国人名是一种冒犯性的行为。(156字)

附录 2

全国大学英语六级考试
翻译题型指南及真题演练

  全国大学英语六级考试是大学阶段的重要考试之一，其中翻译题既考查学生的外语基本功，又考查学生的双语综合运用能力，因此是整场考试中至关重要的一个部分。六级翻译题考查学生把汉语所承载的信息用英语表达出来的能力，翻译语篇内容涉及中国的历史、文化、经济、社会发展等。2013年六级考试改革以来，"梅兰竹菊""中国园林""丝绸之路""传统佳节"和"大好河山"等译题秉承了六级翻译样题的整体风格，汉译英部分体现出浓郁的"中国风"特点。下面为广大考生整理考试简介、评分标准、考试技巧、真题演练等相关信息。请大家认真观看解析视频，一起了解探究，不断提高。

全国大学英语六级考试翻译题型简介

考题篇幅	180—200 个汉字
答题时间	30 分钟
分值占比	15%（满分 15 分）
考查要求	1) 准确：用词准确，句子表达含义准确，避免漏译、错译； 2) 通顺：译文符合英语的语法结构和语用习惯，逻辑通顺
注意事项	1) 合理分配时间：用 1～2 分钟通读原文，把握语篇所属领域，调动相关中英词汇及该领域的背景知识；预留 3 分钟用于最后的检查； 2) 遇到个别生僻词，不要停留过长的时间，尽量根据上下文的逻辑关系和词性判断该词在句子中的成分，推测词汇的大致含义； 3) 遇到结构复杂、篇幅较长的句子，尽量避免机械地直译，必须在理解原文的基础上重新组织译文语序，灵活运用学过的句式转换、词性转换等翻译技巧，提高译文质量； 4) 由于翻译篇幅较长，需要学生平时加强训练，提高双语水平和思维能力，快速理清语内衔接及逻辑关系，加快翻译速度； 5) 翻译完成后，通读译文，比对原义，确保译义忠实于原文，对表达不地道的译文进行修改和润色，避免"翻译腔"，提高译文可读性

全国大学英语六级考试翻译题型评分标准

档次		分值	译文描述
优秀	评分总则	13—15 分	译文准确表达了原文的意思。用词贴切，行文流畅，基本上无语言错误，仅有个别小错
	评分细则	15 分	有 2 处不明显的小错（冠词、单复数、时态、介词、用词不贴切等）
		14 分	有 5 处不明显的小错（冠词、单复数、时态、介词、用词不贴切等）
		13 分	有 7 处不明显的小错（冠词、单复数、时态、介词、用词不贴切等）

(续表)

档次		分值	译文描述
良好	评分总则	10—12分	译文基本上表达了原文的意思。结构较清晰,文字通顺、连贯,无重大语言错误
	评分细则	12分	有1处明显语言错误
		11分	有3处明显语言错误
		10分	有4处明显语言错误
及格	评分总则	7—9分	译文勉强表达了原文的意思。译文勉强连贯,用词欠准确,语言错误相当多,其中有些是严重语言错误
	评分细则	9分	5个句子正确或基本正确
		8分	4个句子正确或基本正确
		7分	3个句子正确或基本正确
不及格	评分总则	4—6分	译文仅表达了一小部分原文的意思。译文连贯性差,用词不准确,有相当多的严重语言错误
	评分细则	6分	内容基本表达,有2个句子正确
		5分	内容基本表达,有1个句子正确
		4分	没有1个正确句子,但有3个句子有小错
	评分总则	0—3分	译文支离破碎。除个别词语或句子,绝大部分文字没有表达原文意思;或未作答
	评分细则	3分	内容勉强表达,但所有句子都有错误或严重错误;严重错误少
		2分	内容勉强表达,严重错误多
		1分	内容勉强表达,严重错误极多
		0分	未作答,或只有几个孤立的词,或译文与原文毫不相关。根据关键词"创作的翻译",不给分

真 题 演 练

1. 中国越来越重视公共图书馆,并鼓励人们充分加以利用。新近公布的统计数字表明,中国的公共图书馆数量在逐年增长。许多图书馆通过翻新和扩建,为读者创造了更为安静、舒适的环境。大型公共图书馆不仅提供种类繁多的参考资料,而且定期举办讲座、展览等活动。近年来,也出现了许多数字图书馆,从而节省了存放图书所需的空间。一些图书馆还推出了自助服务系统,使读者借书还书更加方便,进一步满足了读者的需求。(190字)

2. 洞庭湖位于湖南省东北部,面积很大,但湖水很浅。洞庭湖是长江的蓄洪池,湖的大小很大程度上取决于季节变化。湖北和湖南两省因其与湖的相对位置而得名:湖北意为"湖的北边",而湖南则为"湖的南边"。洞庭湖作为龙舟赛的发源地,在中国文化中享有盛名。据说龙舟赛始于洞庭湖东岸,为的是搜寻楚国爱国诗人屈原的遗体。龙舟赛与洞庭湖及周边的美景,每年都吸引着成千上万来自全国和世界各地的游客。(185字)

3. 过去,拥有一辆私家车对大部分中国人而言是件奢侈的事。如今,私家车在中国随处可见。汽车成了人们生活中不可或缺的一部分,他们不仅开车上下班,还经常驾车出游。有些城市的汽车增长速度过快,以至于交通拥堵和停车位不足的问题日益严峻。这些城市的市政府不得不出台新规,限制上路汽车的数量。由于空气污染日益严重,现在越来越多的人选择购买新能源汽车,中国政府也采取了一些措施,支持新能源汽车的发展。(190字)

4. 中国目前拥有世界上最大最快的高速铁路网。高铁列车的运行速度还将继续提升,更多的城市将修建高铁站。高铁大大缩短了人们出行的时间。相对飞机而言,由于基本不受天气或交通管制的影响,高铁列车的突出优势在于准时。高铁极大地改变了中国人的生活方式。如今,高铁已经成了很多人商务旅行的首选交通工具。越来越多的人也在假日乘高铁外出旅游。还有不少年轻人选择在一个城市工作而在邻近城市居住,每天乘高铁上下班。(194字)

5. 梅花位居中国十大名花之首,源于中国南方,已有三千多年的栽培和种植历史。隆冬时节,五颜六色的梅花不畏严寒,迎着风雪傲然绽放。在中国传统文化中,梅花象征着坚强、纯洁、高雅,激励人们不畏艰难、砥砺前行。自古以来,许多诗人和画家从梅花中获取灵感,创作了无数不朽的作品。普通大众也都喜爱梅花,春节期间常用于家庭装饰。南京市已将梅花定为市花,每年举办梅花节,成千上万的人冒着严寒到梅花山踏雪赏梅。(192字)

6. 牡丹花色艳丽,形象高雅,象征着和平与繁荣,因而在中国有"花中之王"的美誉。中国许多地方都培育和种植牡丹。千百年来,人们创作了许多诗歌和绘画赞美牡丹。唐代时期,牡丹在皇家园林普遍种植并被誉为国花,因而特别风行。10世纪时,洛阳古城成为牡丹栽培中心,而且这一地位一直保持到今天。现在,成千上万的国内外游客蜂拥到洛阳参加一年一度的牡丹节,欣赏洛阳牡丹的独特之美,同时探索九朝古都的历史。(187字)

7. 成语是汉语中一种独特的表达方式,大多由四个汉字组成。它们高度简练且形式固定,但通常能形象地表达深刻的含义。成语大多来源于中国古代的文学作品,通常与某些神话、传说或者历史事件有关。如果不知道某个成语的出处,就很难理解其确切含义。因此,学习成语有助于人们更好地理解中国传统文化。成语在日常会话和文学创作中广泛使用。恰当使用成语可以使一个人的语言更具表现力,交流更有效。(183字)

8. 汉语目前是世界上用作本族语使用人数最多的语言。汉语与西方语言的一个重要区别在于它是方块字,不是以字母构成的。汉语是现存仍在使用的最古老的书写系统。在中国,来自不同地区的人可能听不懂对方的方言,但由于汉字有统一的书写形式,他们交流起来几乎没有任何困难。汉语历史上对团结中华民族发挥了重要作用。今天,随着中国经济的快速增长和全球影响力的增强,越来越多其他国家的人也开始学习汉语。(188字)

9. 近年来,中国越来越多的博物馆免费向公众开放。博物馆展览次数和参观人数都明显增长。在一些广受欢迎的博物馆门前,排长队已很常见。这些博物馆必须采取措施限制参观人数。如今,展览形式越来越多样。一些大型博物馆利用多媒体和虚拟现实等先进技术,使展览更具吸引力。不少博物馆还举办在线展览,人们可在网上观赏珍稀展品。然而,现场观看展品的体验对大多数参观者还是更具吸引力。(178字)

10. 中国的创新正以前所未有的速度蓬勃发展。为了在科学技术上尽快赶超发达国家,中国近年来大幅度增加了研究开发资金。中国的大学和研究所正在积极开展创新研究,这些研究覆盖了从大数据到生物化学,从新能源到机器人等各类高科技领域。它们还与各地的科技园合作,使创新成果商业化。与此同时,无论在产品还是商业模式上,中国企业家也在努力争做创新的先锋,以适应国内外消费市场不断变化和增长的需求。(188字)

附录3

全国研究生入学考试翻译考题指南及真题演练

翻译是全国研究生入学考试英语考题中两大主观题型之一。翻译对于广大考研学子而言,一直是个难以攻克的痛点。考研英语的翻译题为英译中,多数摘自阅读理解原文中的长难句,例如篇幅较长、语法结构复杂的句子,通常也是阅读理解过程中的"拦路虎"。可见,想要在翻译部分得高分,考生首先必须具备较强的英语阅读功底,在此基础上再下点功夫掌握一些翻译技巧,也就迎刃而解了。

根据考试大纲,考研英语共5小题,每题2分,共计10分。评分标准如下:

	标准描述	备注
1	如果句子译文明显扭曲了原文的意思,该句得分最多不超过0.5分	在实际评分过程中,阅卷人会将一个句子分成3—4个采分点,然后按点给分
2	如果考生就一个题目提供了两个或两个以上的译文,且均正确,给分;若其中一个译法有错,按错误译文给分	
3	译文的错别字不个别计分,按整篇累计扣分。在不影响意思的前提下,满三个中文错别字扣0.5分,没有0.25分	

准确理解原文是完成英汉翻译任务的前提条件和本质要求。吕叔湘先生曾经指出,要做好翻译工作,必须对原文有彻底的了解,而要了解原文,必须通过三道关:第一关是词汇语法关,第二关是俗语关,第三关是字典也帮不了你的种种知识。可见,广大考生只有不断积累词汇、语法、翻译技巧等外语知识储备,并不断扩大知识面,丰富自己的百科认知储备,才能在翻译中得心应手。

关于考研中的翻译,我们建议考生按照"通读全文→文本理解→信息提取→译文组织→译文复查"等步骤,有条不紊地完成翻译:

一、通读全文。阅读理解是读者从原有的认知结构和记忆体系中提取信息,并与输入信息融合加工的一个积极互动和信息匹配的过程。文章是一个有机整体,画线部分也不是孤立存在的,句子与句子之间通过逻辑关系相互衔接、相互支撑,每个句子都围绕着主旨展开。因此,在着手翻译画线部分之前建议考生先通读全文,从整体上了解文章的整体内容和思路框架,准确把握作者的写作意图和表达主题,只有这样才能更好地理清画线部分与其他部分之间的语法与逻辑关系。

二、文本理解。心理语言学关于大脑词汇的研究表明,输入信息与记忆信息匹配的程度越高,理解的程度也就越高。如果记忆信息缺失,那么理解就会遇到障碍,导致考生"云里雾里",摸不着方向;如果记忆信息出错,那么考生的理解会产生偏差,即理解不合常理或不符合原文。建议考生不仅要理解句子表层意思，还要根据上下文理解特定语境中的深层含义。尤其是画线句子中的代词，其所指代的含义可能出现在前后未画线的文本中，因此文本理解离不开对全文的回顾与联系。

三、信息提取。画线部分是翻译的重点，因此需要深入分析，提取重要信息。例如找出句中的意群，快速切分，理清各个意群的语法逻辑功能。一个意群就是一个信息点，翻译时要着眼于这些信息点，不要遗漏，这样有助于提高译文的完整性。分析画线部分的句法结构，划分主句和从句的起止，理清句子的主干和从属成分之间的逻辑关系，把握句子的主要信息，这些也是翻译中的重要采分点；还要注意句子中是否有省略的写法，英语惯用省略手法，翻译时需要把省略的信息补充完整。

四、译文组织。在综合了解全文主旨和上下文的基础上，需要以意群为单位开展快速直译。翻译阶段考生需要综合运用各种翻译方法，尽量忠实再现原文的意义与风格。这个环节承上启下，是能否完成翻译任务的关键。直译，并非逐字对应着开展机械的翻译，建议考生着眼于"意群"，将脑子里第一时间反应出的汉语词汇和短语进行粗略的匹配和组装。选词要准确，句子结构要符合汉语的表达习惯。画线部分有时候包含一些成语、谚语、俗语之类的固定结构，这些也往往是重要的考点和采分点。建议考生不要望文生义、生搬硬套，否则容易造成偏差或错译。一方面，考生平时需要多积累一些固定结构；另一方面，考场上必须沉着冷静，根据上下文合理推测，尽可能接近原文的意思。直译时要注意规避大面积的语序混乱现象，可按照语感自动做一些调整，避免低级的书写错误，重点注意一词多义和易产生歧义的意群。

五、译文复查。由于英汉两种语言在文法及表达方式上存在诸多差异，完全直译往往无法高质量地完成翻译任务。建议考生通读直译的译本，然后判断是否通顺、自然。如果可行，那么就采取直译；如果感觉译文读起来生硬、别扭、不流畅，那么就需要借助本教材所讲授的词性转换、增词减词、分译合译、语序转换、语态转化等翻译技巧对译文进行调整，适当采取意译的方式。最后，润色，调整，成文。这个再加工的环节对于翻译而言至关重要，其重要性决不亚于直译的过程。需要考生在准确理解画线部分句子含义的基础上，在头脑中打破原文语言结构的束缚，重新整合，重新组建，用通顺的汉语还原英语原句的含义。

请大家认真观看解析视频，一起了解探究考研英语中的翻译，积累有效的攻略和技巧。

真 题 演 练

1. (1) <u>World war was the watershed event for higher education in modern Western societies. Those societies came out of the war with levels of enrollment that had been roughly constant at 3—5% of the relevant age groups during the decades before the war.</u> But after the war, great social and political changes arising out of the successful war against Fascism created a growing demand in European and American economies

for increasing numbers of graduates with more than a secondary school education. (2) And the demand that rose in those societies for entry to higher education extended to groups and social classes that had not thought of attending a university before the war. These demands resulted in a very rapid expansion of the systems of higher education, beginning in the 1960s and developing very rapidly (though unevenly) during the 1970s and 1980s.

The growth of higher education manifests itself in at least three quite different ways, and these in turn have given rise to different sets of problems. There was first the rate of growth: (3) in many counties of Western Europe, the numbers of students in higher education doubled within five-year periods during the 1960s and doubled again in seven, eight or ten years by the middle of the 1970s. Second growth obviously affected the absolute size both of systems and individual institutions. And third growth was reflected in changes in the proportion of the relevant age group enrolled in institutions of higher education.

Each of these manifestations of growth carried its own peculiar problems in its wake. For example, a high growth rate placed great strains on the existing structures of governance, of administration, and above all of socialization. When a faculty or department grows from, say, five to twenty members within three or four years, (4) and when the new staff predominantly young men and women fresh from postgraduate study, they largely define the norms of academic life in that faculty. And if the postgraduate student population also grows rapidly and there is loss of a close apprenticeship relationship between faculty members and students, the student culture becomes the chief socializing force for new postgraduate students, with consequences for the intellectual and academic life of the institution — this was seen in America as well as in France, Italy, West Germany, and Japan. (5) High growth rates increased the chances for academic innovation, and they also weakened the forms and processes by which teachers and students are admitted into a community of scholars during periods of stability or slow growth. In the 1960s and 1970s, European universities saw marked changes in their governance arrangements, with empowerment of junior faculty and to some degree of students as well.

2. Following the explosion of creativity in Florence during the 14th century known as the Renaissance, the modern world saw a departure from what it had once known. It turned from God and the authority of the Roman Catholic Church and instead favoured a more humanistic approach to being. Renaissance ideas had spread

throughout Europe well into the 17th century, with the arts and sciences flourishing extraordinarily among those with a more logical disposition. (1) With the Church's teachings and ways of thinking being eclipsed by the Renaissance, the gap between the Medieval and modern periods had been bridged, leading to new and unexplored intellectual territories.

During the Renaissance, the great minds of Nicolaus Copernicus, Johannes Kepler and Galileo Galilei demonstrated the power of scientific study and discovery. (2) Before each of their revelations, many thinkers at the time had sustained more ancient ways of thinking, including the Ptolemaic and Aristotlean geocentric view that the Earth was at the centre of our universe. Copernicus theorised in 1543 that in actual fact, all of the planets that we knew of revolved not around the Earth, but the Sun, a system that was later upheld by Galileo at his own expense. Offering up such a theory during a time of high tension between scientific and religious minds was branded as heresy, and any such heretics that continued to spread these lies were to be punished by imprisonment or even death. Galileo was excommunicated by the Church and imprisoned for life for his astronomical observations and his support of the heliocentric principle.

(3) Despite attempts by the Church to suppress this new generation of logicians and rationalists, more explanations for how the universe functioned were being made, and at a rate that the people — including the Church — could no longer ignore. It was with these great revelations that a new kind of philosophy founded in reason was born.

The Church's long-standing dogma was losing the great battle for truth to rationalists and scientists. This very fact embodied the new ways of thinking that swept through Europe during most of the 17th century. (4) As many took on the duty of trying to integrate reasoning and scientific philosophies into the world, the Renaissance was over and it was time for a new era — the Age of Reason.

The 17th and 18th centuries were times of radical change and curiosity. Scientific method, reductionism and the questioning of Church ideals was to be encouraged, as were ideas of liberty, tolerance and progress. (5) Such actions to seek knowledge and to understand what information we already knew were captured by the Latin phrase "sapere aude" or "dare to know", after Immanuel Kant used it in his essay *An Answer to the Question: What is Enlightenment*? It was the purpose and responsibility of great minds to go forth and seek out the truth, which they believed to be founded in knowledge.

3. It was only after I started to write a weekly column about the medical journals, and began to read scientific papers from beginning to end, that I realized just how bad much of the medical literature frequently was. I came to recognize various signs of a bad paper: the kind of paper that purports to show that people who eat more than one kilo of broccoli a week were 1.17 times more likely than those who eat less to suffer late in life from pernicious anaemia. (1) <u>There is a great deal of this kind of nonsense in the medical journals which, when taken up by broadcasters and the press, generates both health scares and short-lived dietary enthusiasms.</u>

Why is so much bad science published? A recent paper, titled "The Natural Selection of Bad Science", published on the Royal Society's open science website, attempts to answer this intriguing and important question. It says that the problem is not merely that people do bad science, but that our current system of career advancement positively encourages it. What is important is not truth, but publication, which has become almost an end in itself. There has been a kind of inflationary process at work: (2) <u>nowadays anyone applying for a research post has to have published twice the number of papers that would have been required for the same post only 10 years ago.</u> Never mind the quality, then, count the number.

(3) <u>Attempts have been made to curb this tendency, for example, by trying to incorporate some measure of quality as well as quantity into the assessment of an applicant's papers.</u> This is the famed citation index, that is to say the number of times a paper has been quoted elsewhere in the scientific literature, the assumption being that an important paper will be cited more often than one of small account. (4) <u>This would be reasonable if it were not for the fact that scientists can easily arrange to cite themselves in their future publications, or get associates to do so for them in return for similar favours.</u>

Boiling down an individual's output to simple metrics, such as number of publications or journal impacts, entails considerable savings in time, energy and ambiguity. Unfortunately, the long-term costs of using simple quantitative metrics to assess researcher merit are likely to be quite great. (5) <u>If we are serious about ensuring that our science is both meaningful and reproducible, we must ensure that our institutions encourage that kind of science.</u>

4. Shakespeare's life time was coincident with a period of extraordinary activity and achievement in the drama. (1) <u>By the date of his birth, Europe was witnessing the passing of the religious drama that had held its course for some five centuries, and the</u>

creation of new and mixed forms under the incentive of classical tragedy and comedy. These new forms were at first mainly written by scholars and performed by amateurs, but in England, as everywhere else in western Europe, the growth of a class of professional actors was threatening to make the drama popular, whether it should be new or old, classical or medieval, literary or farcical. Court, school organizations of amateurs, and the traveling actors were all rivals in supplying a widespread desire for dramatic entertainment; and (2) <u>no boy who went to a grammar school could be ignorant that the drama was a form of literature which gave glory to Greece and Rome and might yet bring honor to England.</u>

When Shakespeare was twelve years old, the first public playhouse was built in London. For a time literature showed no interest in this public stage. Plays aiming at literary distinction were written for school or court, or for the choir boys of St. Paul's and the royal chapel, who, however, gave plays in public as well as at court. (3) <u>But the professional companies prospered in their permanent theaters, and university men with literature ambitions were quick to turn to these theaters as offering a means of livelihood.</u> By the time Shakespeare was twenty-five, Lyly, Peele, and Greene had made comedies that were at once popular and literary; Kyd had written a tragedy that crowded the pit; and Marlowe had brought poetry and genius to triumph on the common stage — where they had played no part since the death of Euripides. (4) <u>A native literary drama had been created, its alliance with the public playhouses established, and at least some of its great traditions had been begun.</u>

The development of the Elizabethan drama for the next twenty-five years is of exceptional interest to students of literary history, for in this brief period we may trace the beginning, growth, blossoming, and decay of many kinds of plays, and of many great careers. We are amazed today at the mere number of plays produced, as well as by the number of dramatists writing at the same time for this London of two hundred thousand inhabitants. (5) <u>To realize how great the dramatic activity was, we must remember further that hosts of plays have been lost, and that probably there is no author of note whose entire work has survived.</u>

5. The growth of the use of English as the world's primary language for international communication has obviously been continuing for several decades. (1) <u>But even as the number of English speakers expands further there are signs that the global predominance of the language may fade within the foreseeable future.</u> Complex international, economic, technological and cultural change could start to diminish the

leading position of English as the language of the world market, and UK's interests which enjoy advantage from the breath of English usage would consequently face new pressures. Those realistic possibilities are highlighted in the study presented by David Graddol.

(2) <u>His analysis should therefore end any self-contentedness among those who may believe that the global position of English is so stable that the young generation of the United Kingdom do not need additional language capabilities.</u>

David Graddol concludes that monoglot English graduates face a bleak economic future as qualified multilingual youngsters from other countries are proving to have a competitive advantage over their British counterparts in global companies and organizations. Alongside that, (3) <u>many countries are introducing English into the primary-school curriculum but British schoolchildren and students do not appear to be gaining greater encouragement to achieve fluency in other languages.</u>

If left to themselves, such trends will diminish the relative strength of the English language in international education markets as the demand for educational resources in languages, such as Spanish, Arabic or Mandarin grows and international business process outsourcing in other language such as Japanese, French and German, spreads.

(4) <u>The changes identified by David Graddol all present clear and major challenges to UK's providers of English language teaching to people of other countries and to broader education business sectors.</u> The English language teaching sector directly earns nearly & 1.3 billion for the UK in invisible exports and our other education related sectors earn up to 10 billion a year more. As the international education market expands, the recent slowdown in the number of international students studying in the main English-speaking countries is likely to continue, especially if there are no effective strategic policies to prevent such slippage.

The anticipation of possible shifts in demand provided by this study is significant. (5) <u>It gives a basis to all organizations which seek to promote the learning and the use of English, a basis for planning to meet possibilities of what could be a very different operating environment.</u> That is a necessary and practical approach. In this as in much else, those who wish to influence the future must prepare for it.

6. Mental health is our birthright. (1) <u>We don't have to learn how to be mentally healthy; it is built into us in the same way that our bodies know how to heal a cut or mend a broken bone.</u> Mental health can't be learned, only reawakened. It is like the

immune system of the body, which under stress or through lack of nutrition or exercise can be weakened, but which never leaves us. When we don't understand the value of mental health and we don't know how to gain access to it, mental health will remain hidden from us. (2) <u>Our mental health doesn't really go anywhere; like the sun behind a cloud, it can be temporarily hidden from view, but it is fully capable of being restored in an instant.</u>

Mental health is the seed that contains self-esteem — confidence in ourselves and an ability to trust in our common sense. It allows us to have perspective on our lives — the ability to not take ourselves too seriously, to laugh at ourselves, to see the bigger picture, and to see that things will work out. It's a form of innate or unlearned optimism. (3) <u>Mental health allows us to view others with sympathy if they are having troubles, with kindness if they are in pain, and with unconditional love no matter who they are.</u> Mental health is the source of creativity for solving problems, resolving conflict, making our surroundings more beautiful, managing our home life, or coming up with a creative business idea or invention to make our lives easier. It gives us patience for ourselves and toward others as well as patience while driving, catching a fish, working on our car, or raising a child. It allows us to see the beauty that surrounds us each moment in nature, in culture, in the flow of our daily lives.

(4) <u>Although mental health is the cure-all for living our lives, it is perfectly ordinary as you will see that it has been there to direct you through all your difficult decisions.</u> It has been available even in the most mundane of life situations to show you right from wrong, good from bad, friend from foe. Mental health has commonly been called conscience, instinct, wisdom, common sense, or the inner voice. We think of it simply as a healthy and helpful flow of intelligent thought. (5) <u>As you will come to see, knowing that mental heath is always available and knowing to trust it allow us to slow down to the moment and live life happily.</u>

7. Within the span of a hundred years, in the seventeenth and early eighteenth centuries, a tide of emigration — one of the great folk wanderings of history — swept from Europe to America. (1) <u>This movement, driven by powerful and diverse motivations, built a nation out of a wilderness and, by its nature, shaped the character and destiny of an uncharted continent.</u>

(2) <u>The United States is the product of two principal forces — the immigration of European peoples with their varied ideas, customs, and national characteristics and the impact of a new country which modified these traits.</u> Of necessity, colonial America was

a projection of Europe. Across the Atlantic came successive groups of Englishmen, Frenchmen, Germans, Scots, Irishmen, Dutchmen, Swedes, and many others who attempted to transplant their habits and traditions to the new world. (3) <u>But, the force of geographic conditions peculiar to America, the interplay of the varied national groups upon one another, and the sheer difficulty of maintaining old-world ways in a raw, new continent caused significant changes.</u> These changes were gradual and at first scarcely visible. But the result was a new social pattern which, although it resembled European society in many ways, had a character that was distinctly American.

(4) <u>The first shiploads of immigrants bound for the territory which is now the United States crossed the Atlantic more than a hundred years after the fifteenth- and sixteenth-century explorations of North America.</u> In the meantime, thriving Spanish colonies had been established in Mexico, the West Indies, and South America. These travelers to North America came in small, unmercifully overcrowded craft. During their six- to twelve-week voyage, they subsisted on meager rations. Many of the ships were lost in storms, many passengers died of disease, and infants rarely survived the journey. Sometimes tempests blew the vessels far off their course, and often calm brought interminable delay.

To the anxious travelers the sight of the American shore brought almost inexpressible relief. Said one chronicler, "The air at twelve leagues' distance smelt as sweet as a new-blown garden." The colonists' first glimpse of the new land was a vista of dense woods. (5) <u>The virgin forest with its richness and variety of trees was a real treasure-house which extended from Maine all the way down to Georgia in the south.</u> Here was abundant fuel and lumber. Here was the raw material of houses and furniture, ships and potash, dyes and naval stores.

8. Music means different things to different people and sometimes even different things to the same person at different moments of his life. It might be poetic, philosophical, sensual, or mathematical, but in any case it must, in my view, have something to do with the soul of the human being. Hence it is metaphysical; but the means of expression is purely and exclusively physical: sound. I believe it is precisely this permanent coexistence of metaphysical message through physical means that is the strength of music. (1) <u>It is also the reason why when we try to describe music with words, all we can do is articulate our reactions to it, and not grasp music itself.</u>

Beethoven's importance in music has been principally defined by the revolutionary nature of his compositions. He freed music from hitherto prevailing conventions of harmony and structure. Sometimes I feel in his late works a will to break all signs of continuity. The music is abrupt and seemingly disconnected, as in the last piano sonata. In musical expression, he did not feel restrained by the weight of convention. (2) <u>By all accounts he was a freethinking person, and a courageous one, and I find courage an essential quality for the understanding, let alone the performance, of his works.</u>

This courageous attitude in fact becomes a requirement for the performers of Beethoven's music. His compositions demand the performer to show courage, for example in the use of dynamics. (3) <u>Beethoven's habit of increasing the volume with an extreme intensity and then abruptly following it with a sudden soft passage was only rarely used by composers before him.</u>

Beethoven was a deeply political man in the broadest sense of the word. He was not interested in daily politics, but concerned with questions of moral behavior and the larger questions of right and wrong affecting the entire society. (4) <u>Especially significant was his view of freedom, which, for him, was associated with the rights and responsibilities of the individual: he advocated freedom of thought and of personal expression.</u>

Beethoven's music tends to move from chaos to order as if order were an imperative of human existence. For him, order does not result from forgetting or ignoring the disorders that plague our existence; order is a necessary development, an improvement that may lead to the Greek ideal of spiritual elevation. It is not by chance that the Funeral March is not the last movement of the Eroica Symphony, but the second, so that suffering does not have the last word. (5) <u>One could interpret much of the work of Beethoven by saying that suffering is inevitable, but the courage to fight it renders life worth living.</u>

9. It is speculated that gardens arise from a basic human need in the individuals who made them: the need for creative expression. There is no doubt that gardens evidence an irrepressible urge to create, express, fashion, and beautify and that self-expression is a basic human urge; (1) <u>yet when one looks at the photographs of the garden created by the homeless, it strikes one that, for all their diversity of styles, these gardens speak of various other fundamental urges, beyond that of decoration and creative expression.</u>

One of these urges has to do with creating a state of peace in the midst of turbulence, a "still point of the turning world," to borrow a phrase from T. S. Eliot. (2) A sacred place of peace, however crude it may be, is a distinctly human need, as opposed to shelter, which is a distinctly animal need. This distinction is so much so that where the latter is lacking, as it is for these unlikely gardens, the former becomes all the more urgent. Composure is a state of mind made possible by the structuring of one's relation to one's environment. (3) The gardens of the homeless, which are in effect homeless gardens, introduce form into an urban environment where it either didn't exist or was not discernible as such. In so doing they give composure to a segment of the inarticulate environment in which they take their stand.

Another urge or need that these gardens appear to respond to, or to arise from, is so intrinsic that we are barely ever conscious of its abiding claims on us. When we are deprived of green, of plants, of trees, (4) most of us give in to a demoralization of spirit which we usually blame on some psychological conditions, until one day we find ourselves in a garden and feel the oppression vanish as if by magic. In most of the homeless gardens of New York City the actual cultivation of plants is unfeasible, yet even so the compositions often seem to represent attempts to call forth the spirit of plant and animal life, if only symbolically, through a clumplike arrangement of materials, an introduction of colors, small pools of water, and a frequent presence of petals or leaves as well as of stuffed animals. On display here are various fantasy elements whose reference, at some basic level, seems to be the natural world. (5) It is this implicit or explicit reference to nature that fully justifies the use of the word *garden*, though in a "liberated" sense, to describe these synthetic constructions. In them we can see biophilia — a yearning for contact with nonhuman life — assuming uncanny representational forms.

10. Since the days of Aristotle, a search for universal principles has characterized the scientific enterprise. In some ways, this quest for commonalities defines science. Newton's laws of motion and Darwinian evolution each bind a host of different phenomena into a single explicatory framework.

(1) In physics, one approach takes this impulse for unification to its extreme, and seeks a theory of everything — a single generative equation for all we see. It is becoming less clear, however, that such a theory would be a simplification, given the dimensions and universes that it might entail. Nonetheless, unification of sorts remains a major goal.

This tendency in the natural sciences has long been evident in the social sciences too. (2) Here, Darwinism seems to offer justification, for if all humans share common origins, it seems reasonable to suppose that cultural diversity could also be traced to more constrained beginnings. Just as the bewildering variety of human courtship rituals might all be considered forms of sexual selection, perhaps the world's languages, music, social and religious customs and even history are governed by universal features. (3) To filter out what is unique from what is shared might enable us to understand how complex cultural behavior arose and what guides it in evolutionary or cognitive terms.

That, at least, is the hope. But a comparative study of linguistic traits published online today supplies a reality check. Russell Gray at the University of Auckland and his colleagues consider the evolution of grammars in the light of two previous attempts to find universality in language.

The most famous of these efforts was initiated by Noam Chomsky, who suggested that humans are born with an innate language acquisition capacity that dictates a universal grammar. A few generative rules are then sufficient to unfold the entire fundamental structure of a language, which is why children can learn it so quickly.

(4) The second, by Joshua Greenberg, takes a more empirical approach to universality, identifying traits (particularly in word order) shared by many languages which are considered to represent biases that result from cognitive constraints.

Gray and his colleagues have put them to the test by examining four family trees that between them represent more than 2,000 languages. (5) Chomsky's grammar should show patterns of language change that are independent of the family tree or the pathway tracked through it, whereas Greenbergian universality predicts strong co-dependencies between particular types of word-order relations. Neither of these patterns is borne out by the analysis, suggesting that the structures of the languages are lineage-specific and not governed by universals.

附录 4

口译加油站

1 礼仪接待

口译中礼仪接待类的讲话一般包括祝酒词、各种场合的开幕词和闭幕词、接待宾客的欢迎词和答谢词等。正式的礼仪接待类讲话通常包括称呼、感谢或祝贺等客套话、正文、结尾等几个部分。请大家观看"礼仪接待"口译实践指导视频,了解相关知识。

> 听英文,完成口译实践训练,并大声朗读原文,注意口译技巧和译文效果,熟练掌握英汉互译的表达式。

A:请问,___1___?

B:是的,我就是。您一定是郑女士吧?

A:嗯,是的是的。欢迎您来到上海! ___2___。

B:见到您真高兴。___3___。

A:万分荣幸。我也很高兴见到您。旅途顺利吗?

B:还不错。

A: ___4___。

B:我一直期待着参观你们的国家,现在终于如愿了。

A:您对我们的国家了解得越多,就会越喜欢这里。___5___。

B:我万分期待。

A: ___6___。一会儿他会来宾馆见您。___7___。

B:谢谢,票子给您。___8___。

A:乐意为您效劳。

A. 今天由我到这里来接您

B. 刘先生目前正在参加一个重要的会议

C. 在此期间,请您多多关照啊

D. 您是在等候环球商务公司的刘先生吗

E. 您是来自东方电子公司的米勒先生吗

F. 请把您的行李票给我,我去帮您取行李

G. 我已经从刘先生那里了解到您的很多情况
H. 我们国家地大物博，历史悠久，相信您一定会喜欢这里
I. 感谢您亲自来机场接我
J. 真诚地希望您在这里度过愉快的时光

2　商务交流

商务口译具有典型的特点，例如商务交流活动往往涉及进出口贸易、商务谈判、生产管理、可行性研究、财务与会计、劳资关系、市场调研等具体的交易和程序。可见，商务交流活动的多样性给商务口译带来了很大的挑战。请大家观看"商务交流"口译实践指导视频，了解相关知识。

> 听英文，完成口译实践训练，并大声朗读原文，注意口译技巧和译文效果，熟练掌握英汉互译的表达式。

A：你的意思是说　1　？
B：就是这个意思。　2　。
A：我们给其他地区代理的佣金通常是5%～7%。
B：但我方市场对你方的产品仍然不太了解，　3　。
A：如果提供你方10%的佣金，那么对于我方而言利润所剩无几了。你看，　4　，我们跟加拿大所有的批发商、连锁商店和分销商都保持着良好的关系。
B：　5　。
A：感谢你们乐意推销我方产品的意愿，对你们过去两年的的销售表现我们也非常满意。但说实在的，　6　。
B：如果我们得到独家代理权，　7　。
A：好的，　8　。
B：好，就这么定了。

A. 我们保证销售量可翻一番
B. 如果我们指定你们为代理，你们每年的销售额可以达到100万美元
C. 我们的纺织大楼建的很好
D. 我们在推销过程中需要做很多工作，开销也不是一个小数目
E. 可以通融一下，我们同意支付10%的佣金
F. 我公司在纺织业有良好的声誉
G. 当然我们要求10%的佣金

H. 100万美元的年销售量离独家代理权相差甚远

I. 仅凭100万美元的年销售量还无法确定你们能胜任独家代理的工作

J. 如果指定我们为你们的独家代理,日后你们肯定会觉得这个决定特别明智

3 叙述介绍

口译中叙述介绍类的讲话往往通过陈述事件的起因、经过和结果向听众提供信息,例如在谈话中引用的故事和典故,或者对过去发生的事件的描述、追忆或回顾。请大家观看"叙述介绍"口译实践指导视频,了解相关知识。

> 听英文,完成口译实践训练,并大声朗读原文,注意口译技巧和译文效果,熟练掌握英汉互译的表达式。

季节性情绪紊乱(SAD)指多发于冬季的一种抑郁症,也称"冬季抑郁症"。与其他类型的抑郁症不同的是,__1__——隆冬降临,感觉抑郁;春暖花开,病情好转。血清素是大脑中的一种化学物质,能够影响人的情绪。__2__,其分泌量降低会诱发季节性情绪紊乱。白昼变短同样会扰乱人体生物钟,继而导致褪黑素(____)分泌失衡。由于北方寒冷气候带地区冬季白昼时间很短,__4__。该症状的女性患者多于男性,__5__。

"年关焦虑症"指的是__6__,通常由年度收入不佳、工作和家庭压力引起。__7__。也许你正在为过去一年没能实现既定目标后悔不已,__8__!

A. 而且40岁以下的人群更容易发病

B. 这是由于昼夜长短的季节性变化造成的

C. 调节情绪和睡眠规律的荷尔蒙

D. 但是你还是可以下定决心在来年做得更好

E. 哲学家建议我们应该避免同伴竞争

F. 血清素的分泌受到季节性光照变化的影响

G. 因此季节性情绪紊乱在北方更为常见

H. 这是一种循环性的、反复发生的情绪紊乱

I. 心理专家建议不应盲目攀比

J. 由于年关将至而产生的自责和恐慌心理

4 旅游观光

旅游观光类口译中一个很重要的组成部分就是导游口译,该类口译活动体现出"边导边译、

导译结合"的特点。旅游观光类口译活动涉及面广,例如天文、地理、政治、经济、历史、文化、风俗、宗教等都是常见的话题。请大家观看"旅游观光"口译实践指导视频,了解相关知识。

> 听英文,完成口译实践训练,并大声朗读原文,注意口译技巧和译文效果,熟练掌握英汉互译的表达式。

希腊以其众多的历史遗迹、粉刷成白色的村庄、__1__而闻名遐迩,__2__。但希腊旅游业之所以发达,__3__。通常,__4__。这些岛屿如同镶嵌在希腊半岛周边海域中的一颗颗璀璨的小宝石。每一个岛屿都展现出__5__。

__6__,以古希腊海神波塞冬神庙遗址所在地而闻名。__7__。对于来自希腊雅典的游客来说,这里是最受欢迎的一日游景点。__8__,美不胜收。

A. 你可以在这些岛屿上发现分散着的希腊的美
B. 这些遗址坐落在岬角上,三面环海
C. 阳光灿烂的海滩、诱人的美食和友善的氛围
D. 阳光、沙滩、海风……这里一切宜人
E. 游客慕名而来,从遗址眺望爱琴海的日落
F. 美轮美奂的风景、历史遗迹、夜生活和文化风情
G. 最根本的原因就在于这里的景致实在太迷人了
H. 难怪它能跻身欧洲最热门的旅游度假地之列
I. 你可以在一些星星点点的岛屿上尽享希腊之美
J. 苏尼翁角位于阿提卡半岛最南端

5 论证演说

论证演说类口译一般包括总论、论证过程和结论等几个部分,用以阐明事理,表明观点,常出现在一些正式的场合,例如国际性会议、记者招待会、正式会晤、公众演讲等。该类口译较之其他的语类表现出以下特点:语级较高,表达方式较为正式,论证过程具有很强的逻辑性。请大家观看"论证演说"口译实践指导视频,了解相关知识。

> 听英文,完成口译实践训练,并大声朗读原文,注意口译技巧和译文效果,熟练掌握英汉互译的表达式。

冷战结束以来,__1__。__2__的呼声日益高涨。中国对__3__表示愤慨。靖国神社供奉着__4__。小泉的参拜__5__。中国人民决不能__6__。__7__才是对待历史问题的正确态度。凡事都应有一个是非判断,__8__。

A. 接受日本领导人的这一行为
B. 沾满中国和其他亚洲人民鲜血的甲级战犯的牌位
C. 一个人应该为自己的错误负责
D. 世界形势总体趋向缓和
E. 日本领导人破坏了中日两国的友好关系
F. 世界各国人民要和平、求稳定、谋发展
G. 日本首相小泉参拜靖国神社
H. 以史为鉴、面向未来
I. 人无是非,难以立信;国无是非,难以立世
J. 破坏了中日两国邦交的政治基础

6 融会贯通

口译活动是一个综合性的思维加工过程,常用的笔译技巧在口译过程中也都是适用的。因此,我们可以利用所学的增词法、减词法、词性转换法、分译法、合译法、转序法、语态转换法等技巧,融会贯通,综合运用,举一反三,提高口译的效果。请大家观看"融会贯通"口译实践指导视频,了解相关知识。

> 听英文,完成口译实践训练,并大声朗读原文,注意口译技巧和译文效果,熟练掌握英汉互译的表达式。

____1____,让智能手机用户知道____2____。这项技术将____3____。如果某人新冠病毒检测呈阳性,____4____。这些公共卫生应用程序将____5____。这项技术可以在谷歌安卓手机和苹果 iPhone 手机上使用。两家公司坚称,____6____。智能手机用户必须通过自主申请才能使用这一功能。____7____。新冠病毒阳性患者的个人信息将保持匿名,____8____。

A. 他们何时与新冠病毒感染者有过接触
B. 他们将保护智能手机用户的隐私
C. 依赖于能够发送和接收的蓝牙信号的智能手机
D. 科技巨头苹果公司和谷歌公司将联手打造一个系统
E. 依赖智能手机发送和接收的蓝牙信号
F. 不会对接触者或者苹果公司和谷歌公司公布
G. 向所有在过去 14 天内曾经靠近患者手机的智能手机用户发出警报
H. 该软件不会收集用户的定位数据或身份信息
I. 他可以通过一款应用程序通知公共卫生管理部门
J. 该软件不会收集用户的身体特征数据或个人身份信息

参考答案

Chapter 1　Economy & Management 经济管理

Ⅰ.（略）

Ⅱ.参考译文：

后全球化时代

如今贸易的紧张局势加速了自 2008 年金融危机以来的经济转型。相对全球国内生产总值而言，跨境投资、贸易、银行贷款和供应链都处于萎缩或停滞状态。全球化时代俨然被新的经济萧条时代所取代。借用一位荷兰作家创造的术语，我们将其称为"全球化放缓"。

过去十年，全球化发展从光速骤降至蜗速，这其中包含多个原因。运输货物的成本已经停止下降。跨国公司发现，全球扩张十分烧钱，而本土竞争者往往会将其彻底击垮。贸易活动正转向服务领域，而跨国提供服务难度更大。就像剪刀可以装在 20 英尺的集装箱里出口，但出口发型师就没这么容易了。

全新的经济模式将以不同的方式运转。全球化放缓将使得区域集团内部联系更为紧密。北美、欧洲和亚洲的供应链越来越多地就近采购产品。亚洲和欧洲地区开展的贸易大部分为区域内贸易，其贸易份额呈上升态势。去年，亚洲公司对亚洲的出口额超过对美洲的出口额。随着全球规则约束力的减弱，地区性贸易和区域势力形成灵活的体系，正在加强对贸易和投资的控制。

所幸的是，大众生活水平不会受到多大影响。巨大的洲内市场足够促进经济的繁荣。目前约有 12 亿人摆脱了极度贫困，没有理由认为贫困人口比例会再次上升。西方消费者将继续从贸易中获得巨大的净收益。在某些情况下，本可能发生在全球范围的经济深度融合现在更可能发生在区域内部。

然而，全球化放缓有两大弊端。第一，它产生了新的难题。在过去十年里，大多数新兴国家能够缩小与发达国家之间的差距。现在，更多的新兴国家发现，贸易致富的路上困难重重。而且，区域性贸易模式与全球金融体系容易产生摩擦。在全球金融体系中，华尔街和美联储掌握了全球市场的命脉。即使大多数国家的贸易模式与美国的联系越来越少，它们的利率仍会受到美国利率的影响，这会导致金融动荡。现在，美联储不太可能像十年前那样充当全球最后的救星来拯救其他国家。

第二,全球化放缓不会解决全球化带来的问题。西方因自动化被淘汰的蓝领工作岗位不会再度出现。企业将在每个地区人工成本最低的地方雇佣没有专门技能的工人。没有全球合作,气候变化、移民和逃税问题将更难解决。

对大部分人而言,全球化放缓让世界变得更美好,但人们却很少采取措施来减少全球化放缓的代价。全球经济一体化进程中不那么显眼的问题,现在已经加剧发展起来,问题大到使各国开始忽略全球秩序所带来的益处,而现有的解决方案并不能真正解决问题。相比全球化发展,全球化放缓这一模式格局更小,也更不稳定。最终它只会助长不满情绪。

Ⅲ. 参考译文:

Seven Things Great Employers Do

For most people, paid work is unsettling and energy-sapping. Despite employee engagement racing up the priority list of CEOs, our research into workplaces all over the world reveals a sorry state of affairs: workers who are actively disengaged outnumber their engaged colleagues by an overwhelming ratio of 2∶1. The good news is that there are companies out there bucking the trend, and we've discovered how.

Over a five-year timeframe, we studied 32 exemplary companies (collectively employing 600,000 people) across seven industries including hospitality, banking, manufacturing, and hospitals. At these companies, the engaged workers outnumber the actively disengaged ones by a 9-to-1 ratio. To understand what drives that tremendous advantage, we looked for contrasts between them and a much larger set of companies we know to be struggling to turn around bland and uninspiring workplaces.

We found seven characteristics in place at the companies with spirited employees which are notably lacking in the others. Are all of the seven causes of high performance? No doubt at least some of them involve virtuous circles. As a recipe for an engaged workforce, these are ingredients we feel confident in recommending:

1. Have ambitious and passionate leaders who want to improve. Leaders of great workplaces avoid just talking with eloquence about big targets. Instead, they challenge new management models in an earnest and down-to-earth manner and keep practicing to get better at it every day with their own teams.

2. Ensure the basic engagement requirements are met before expecting an inspiring mission to fulfill. When employees know what is expected of them, have what they need to do their jobs, are good fits for their roles, and feel their managers have their backs, they will commit to almost anything the company is trying to accomplish.

3. Never use a downturn as an excuse. With few exceptions, leaders have also had to respond to flat or declining top lines — with structural changes, redundancies, and declining real pay and benefits. They have achieved this by being open, making changes swiftly, communicating constantly, and providing hope.

4. Trust, hold accountable, and relentlessly support their teams. The experiences of inspiring and encouraging employees are effective and rewarding. Strong teams are built only when teams themselves size up the problems facing them and take a hands-on approach to solving them.

5. Have a straightforward and decisive approach to performance management. Indeed, a hallmark of these great workplaces is that they focus on and nurture a sense of recognition. These companies see recognition as a powerful means to develop and stretch employees to new levels of capability. Meanwhile, they see tolerance of mediocrity as the enemy.

6. Do not pursue engagement for its own sake. As it becomes increasingly possible, by means of technology, to measure and track engagement accurately, some companies start "managing to the metric". Nevertheless, real great employers keep their eyes on the outcomes, which actually need greater engagement to achieve.

7. Show solicitude for their employees more. Our research into a representative sample of nearly all the world's adults shows that a job has the potential to be at the heart of a great life, but only if its holder is engaged at work. Copious amount of debate has been devoted to how to make this happen — by making work more fun, funky, and even meaningful — but many companies still fail. The successful examples we studied figured out how to establish emotional connections with their staff.

It isn't easy, but if you focus on the magnificent seven, you too can create a team where people love their work.

Ⅳ. 1. gross domestic product 国内生产总值
2. gross national product 国民生产总值
3. consumer price index 消费者物价指数
4. product price index 生产者物价指数
5. national income 国民收入
6. personal income 个人收入
7. net national product 国民净产值
8. retail price index 零售物价指数

Ⅴ. 1. B 2. A 3. A 4. B 5. A 6. B 7. A 8. B

Ⅵ.

Does Economic Globalization Lead to Larger Cities?
— An Empirical Analysis of Cities in the World and in China

Abstract: Economic globalization and informatization have become two major driving forces for urbanization in the world. However, quantitative research of the relations between economic globalization and urbanization is limited. Based on quantitative analysis, the paper summarizes the features of the world's urban development in a context of economic globalization as follows: ① Obvious stages exist in the growth of metropolises; ② Key areas of metropolitan growth has shifted towards the newly industrialized countries in Asia, Africa and Latin America; ③ Informal urbanization has become a main characteristic of urban morphology; ④ The polarization effect of megacities is greater than the diffusion effect, which has led to a typical dual-urbanization pattern; ⑤ Monopole urbanization, metropolitan growth and network urbanization coexist. The paper also examines two spatial scale at the global and the country (China) level and discusses the relations between economic globalization and the growth of the metropolitan area. The hypothesis that "globalization leads to the development of larger cities" was tested. The study shows that the variability of metropolitan growth in the world is generally lower than that of economic factor mobility; however, in China, the variability of economic factor mobility and metropolis growth are both relatively high.

Keywords: economic globalization; growth of metropolises; empirical analysis

Ⅶ. (略)

Ⅷ.
英译汉练习：
1. 西欧诸国气候**不同**,文化**各异**,山峦、平原、海岸**各具特色**,因此要想把西欧**作为**整体**加以综述**,谈何容易。
2. 他们期待我们欧共体制订出对其问题表示**同情和理解**的援助政策和贸易政策。
3. 联合国文件呼吁以色列**撤出**所占土地,阿拉伯**承认**以色列的生存权,在此基础上**解决**中东冲突。

4. ……民*有*、民*治*、民*享*的政府将永存于世。

汉译英练习：

1. When I arrived in Xuzhou to meet my father, the *sight* of the mess in the courtyard and the *thought* of my grandmother set tears trickling down my cheeks.
2. We small states will discover that capitalism is, by its very nature, *imperialistic* and *exploitative*, and that we become satellites to the capitalist states of Europe and America.
3. The volume of trade has increased tremendously *to the advantage of* both countries.
4. She was wearing a dark red blouse, the rolled up sleeves revealing the *snow* of her arms.

Chapter 2　Language & Culture 语言文化

Ⅰ.（略）

Ⅱ. 参考译文：

消失的语言

1995年，语言学家布鲁斯·康奈尔在喀麦隆开展系列实地考察时发现了一种名为卡塞布的语言。在此之前，尚未有西方人对该语言开展任何研究。当时仅剩一个名叫博贡的人懂卡塞布语，可惜康奈尔抽不出时间去拜访他，遂决定一年后再返回喀麦隆。不料，在抵达喀麦隆的那个初冬，康奈尔却得知博贡早已于11月5日离开了人世。

11月4日，卡塞布语还作为世界上的一种语言留存于世；而在两天后的11月6日，它却突然宣告消亡。这一事件想必在博贡所在的村子里引发了轰动。倘若某个人是某种语言的最后一位传承人，那么同一生活群体中的人往往会认为这个人的存在具有特殊的意义。然而试想，当走出了这个群体，又有谁还会知晓这个特殊的人所代表的语言已经悄然逝去了呢？更遑论为之悼念了。

博贡的故事绝非个例。历史长河中，语言总是随着人类群体的存在而宣告诞生，随着该群体的消亡而销声匿迹。然而，若是用历史的标准来判断，那么当下发生的状况便是不同寻常的。现今世上大约共有6 000种语言，这之中约有一半将在下个世纪走向消亡。

完整的统计数字呈现出骇人听闻之势。有51种语言仅存一位使用者——其中28种语言分布在澳洲。此外，还有3 000多种语言的使用者人数少于10 000人。另有将近5 000种语言仅为人口不足100 000人的群体使用，这着实令人难以置信。另外，全世界96%的语言仅为4%的人口所使用。如此看来，难怪有那么多语言正在濒临消亡。

不论是自然灾害还是文化同化，又抑或种族灭绝，许多因素都能"杀"死一种语言。

1998年7月17日,发生在巴布亚新几内亚的大地震夺走了2 200多人的生命,还致使10 000余人流离失所,几座村子也完完全全地毁于一旦。那么,当幸存者们搬离灾区后,这些原本的村落和村民们世代流传使用的语言在历经流离失所的创伤之后还能幸存下来吗?

即使一个民族没有迁徙或解体,该民族的语言依然会由于文化的同化现象而走向消亡。一开始,人们会感觉有必要使用主导语言。接着,自然而然地步入一段双语并行期。而在最后,双语现象开始衰退,本土语言随之为新兴语言让路,这会引发第三阶段,即在年轻人看来,本土语言的认同感与重要性日益降低。本土语言让位于新兴语言时常伴随着一种心理历程:即认为与主导语言相比,使用本土语言有失面子,之后便逐渐进入了单语言期。

那么,语言的消亡果真是场如此不堪的灾难吗?你或许会说,还能有几百种、甚至几千种语言存活下来,这般境况也便足够了。然而并非如此。我们应当秉持着为动植物物种灭绝时心生担忧的同一份理由,去关切语言的没落问题,因为语言的消亡同样减少了地球上的多样性。回到语言的话题下,我们讨论的不是生物多样性,而是知识和文化的多样性,不过二者是同一个道理。

任何一个物种若想在不同的环境中存活下来,都需要磨练多种多样的技能和特性,这一论断也正为维持语言多样化的必要性提供了有力的支撑。语言中尘封着某个人类群体代代相传的历史演进和一种文化认同感的缩影,除此之外还蕴藏着该群体留下的大量宝贵知识财富,等待世界其他地区的人们去探索发现。

Ⅲ. 参考译文:

Loanwords

English is the "lingua franca" of the modern world, the common language used for science, international business and communication. English is actually a mixture of other languages that has evolved over time based on contact with other cultures. Linguists refer to English as a chain of borrowings that was the result of conquests by foreign invaders. Its adoption of words from so many different languages, known as loanwords, has resulted in it being one of the most diverse languages on the planet.

From about 450 AD to the 11th century, various foreigners invaded England, bringing their languages with them. Britain adapted its language with each invasion, mixing words to create a blended version of many different languages. The most influential languages were: West Germanic after the invasion in 700 AD; Old Norse from the Scandinavian invaders in the 8th and 9th centuries; and most importantly, French and Latin through the Norman Conquest of England in 1066.

English, like any other language, has core words for very familiar everyday things.

Most of these words are of Germanic origin. They are the words that were part of the English brought with them by the Scandinavian settlers. Many of them have not changed very much in the centuries since then, and can be recognized fairly easily. The Norman French invaders left many words of their own language in English, words to do with warfare, government, law, arts and fashion — things that were important to a powerful ruling class. In the sixteenth century, there was a revival of learning and research, and many people shared enthusiasm for the study of Latin and Greek and the culture of past age. There was, at that time, a deliberate effort to make the English vocabulary larger and suitable for a whole range of artistic and scholarly purposes. Of course it seemed natural, in those circumstances, to borrow new words from Latin and Greek. In the following centuries of global exploration and colonial expansion, those who went overseas brought back new products and new experiences, and the words for them too. For example, English started adopting Asian words such as "jungle" and "yoga" during the period of colonialism, when Britain had increased contact with this region.

The continued prevalence of borrowing words across languages demonstrates the close connections different cultures have with one another in our globalized world. The rise of online global media, and the enhanced international communication have led to a greater need for a common language.

Ⅳ. 1. 应用语言学　　　2. 社会语言学　　　3. 心理语言学　　　4. phonetics
　　5. phonology　　　　6. morphology　　　7. syntax　　　　　8. 语义学

Ⅴ. 1. B　2. B　3. B　4. A　5. A　6. B　7. B　8. A

Ⅵ.

The Cognitive Perspective of Systemic Functional Linguistics

Abstract: This paper discusses views concerning cognition, cognitive science and cognitive linguistics held by systemic functional (SF) linguists since the rise of cognitive research in 1980s. It mainly summarizes and reports Halliday's views and comments which appear on various occasions, and occasionally touches upon the views and work held by other SF linguists. The main content covers the role of cognition in SF linguistics, such as the mental process, the three metafunctions, the semantic level, and meaning potential. Based on these, the paper further discusses the relation between cognition and language, semantics, grammar, language learning, semiotics, and cognitive semantic framework. Finally, the writer holds the view that SF linguistics and cognitive linguistics are fellow travelers along the path of the pursuit of knowledge and meaning.

Key words: cognition; meaning; cognitive linguistics; SF linguistics

Ⅶ.（略）

Ⅷ.
英译汉练习：
1. <u>不同</u>国家利用着不同的经济来源；<u>不同</u>民族发展了不同的技能。
2. 应聘兼职女服务员者，有工作经验<u>(比没有工作经验)</u>优先录用。
3. 一看到这一情形，这个金发碧眼的男孩儿立刻<u>在自己胸前划了个十字祈求上帝保佑</u>。
4. 上海市<u>司法当局</u>立即对此事开展调查。

汉译英练习：
1. The newly-introduced drink is ***generally well accepted***.
2. The roofs of this pagoda are constructed of colored glazed tiles of (***different***) yellows and greens.
3. We want a new generation of Chinese conditioned to ***loyalty*** and ***duty***.
4. Courage in excess becomes foolhardiness, affection (***in excess becomes***) weakness, thrift (***in excess becomes***) avarice.

Chapter 3　Sociological Studies 社会研究

Ⅰ.（略）

Ⅱ. 参考译文：

疫　　情

　　当前，新冠疫情持续肆虐全球，世界经济依然面临衰退风险。疫苗是抵御疫情的关键武器。中国反对所谓的"疫苗民族主义"，坚决主张疫苗应成为全球公共产品。中国迄今已向全球160多个国家和国际组织提供了抗疫物资援助，并且正在以不同方式向100多个国家和国际组织提供亟需的疫苗，积极助力全球疫情防控。中国将继续充分发挥自身优势，维护全球抗疫物资供应链稳定，继续积极开展人道主义援助，向有需要的国家提供支持。中国将继续坚定秉持疫苗公共产品的"第一属性"，让更多发展中国家用得上、用得起安全可靠的疫苗。

与此同时,我们将坚持开放合作政策,与各国携手推动世界经济复苏。我们已顺利开启"十四五"规划,加快建设更高水平的开放型经济新体制。一个全面迈向高质量发展的中国,将为各国带来新的发展机遇;而一个持续扩大对外开放的中国,必定为世界经济复苏注入更多动力。

全人类应当成为一个紧密团结的整体。生命与健康,生存与发展,是各国人民都应享有的平等权利。中国将继续高举人类命运共同体旗帜,坚持共商共建共享原则,践行真正的多边主义,捍卫以《联合国宪章》为基础的国际秩序,持续完善全球治理体系,建设人类卫生健康共同体,与各国一道维护世界和平稳定,弥合人类发展鸿沟,与国际社会携手开创更加美好的未来。

Ⅲ. 参考译文:

Population Census

As the world's most populous country as well as the world's second largest economy, China's population censuses have been carried out at a ten-year interval, which serves as a survey of great significance focusing on our national conditions and strengths, as well as aims to reveal the latest cases concerning the size, structure and distribution of our population. China started the seventh Population Census in November 2020, which will provide accurate statistical information for it to embark on the journey of building a modern socialist country in all respects.

Population census is an inherent need for promoting high-quality economic development. Nowadays, China's economy has come to the critical period of development pattern transformation, economic structure optimization and growth impetus transition. Therefore, to timely grasp the basic national situation of population size, structure and distribution and to identify the human resource structure will help us acquire accurate information of the demand composition, urban and rural structure, regional as well as industrial distribution, providing strong support for high-quality economic development and the construction of a modern economic system.

Population census is urgently needed for perfecting the development strategy and policy system for demographic growth, as well as for advancing the long-term balanced growth of population. Since the sixth population census in 2010, we have seen prominent changes to the inner drives and exterior conditions of population growth, demonstrated in a slowdown of the overall size, fluctuating decrease of working-age population as well as continued increase of the aging proportion. To have a full understanding of China's latest population size, structure, distribution and the urban and rural housing situation is at the benefit of learning about changes of population growth, labor supply and migrant population as well as acquiring a better understanding of the size of aging people, which will serve as the basis for making and optimizing policies and measures for future incomes, consumption, education, employment, senior-citizen care, medical care and social insurance, further providing guidance for the layout of educational and medical institutions, building of infrastructure for children and elder people, distribution of industrial and commercial service networks as well as the building of rural and urban roads.

Ⅳ. 1. sociology 社会学　　　　　　　2. political sociology 政治社会学
　　3. educational sociology 教育社会学　4. historical sociology 历史社会学
　　5. cultural sociology 文化社会学　　 6. rural sociology 农村社会学
　　7. urban sociology 都市社会学　　　 8. industrial sociology 工业社会学

Ⅴ. 1. A 2. B 3. A 4. B 5. B 6. B 7. A 8. B

Ⅵ.

On the "Development Mode" of Chinese Urbanization

Abstract: This study looks at the characteristics of the "development mode" of Chinese urbanization from the dual perspectives of its drivers and spatial patterns. The major finding is that the distinctive features of Chinese urbanization include: government leadership, large-scale planning, all-round development, state or collective ownership of land, obvious spatial discontinuities, and a lack of conditions that would allow for spontaneous urbanization by civil society. The "development mode" of Chinese urbanization generally falls into seven catogaries: establishing development areas, building new areas and cities, city expansion, renovation of old cities, setting up central business districts, township industrialization and village industrialization. Although the government-led mode of urbanization demonstrates the creativity and flexibility of the Chinese system, there are still some major questions that urgently need to be studied and resolved: we need to respect objective economic laws and promote benign interactions between the government and the public so as to achieve the equality and justice in urban growth.

Keywords: urbanization; development mode; spatial pattern

Ⅶ.（略）

Ⅷ.
英译汉练习:
1. 但是,这种海军军备竞赛使得自由党政府的**原则无法自圆其说**,也使其**预算捉襟见肘**。
2. 执法部门**如果负责任**,就不能对此不闻不问。
3. 凡是有钱的单身汉,总是想要一位太太。**这已经成了一条举世公认的真理**。
4. **20世纪60年代**,成千上万的黑人**参加**和平示威游行和静坐,**经过**英勇卓绝的斗争,**迫使**南方各州实行联邦政府关于在学校和公共场所废除种族隔离的法律,从而结束了公然歧视黑人的年代。

汉译英练习:
1. It is just great **to** be recognized **for** what you love to do.
2. As for a solely foreign-funded business, the foreign partner provides all the funds and **takes** all the **benefits** as well as **risks**.
3. Solutions of the aging population have to be considered **against a historical background of** slow but substantial changes in **Chinese family structure caused by** rising living standards and family planning.
4. **Having** just left school, **where** they had their place and a target to fulfill and **where** they were cared and esteemed by their peers, those young people **who** do not land that first job **which** they were so eagerly looking forward to have to face up for the first time to unemployment, a situation **for which** no family nor school has prepared them.

Chapter 4 Law & Regulation 法律法规

Ⅰ.(略)

Ⅱ.参考译文:

美国律师事务所之运营模式

雅各比·迈尔斯公司是一家为律师争取打广告的权利而奔走疾呼的先锋。如今,该公司正努力赢得一场新诉讼,用以改变美国法律行业的相关规定。截至9月份,美国法律业在过去12个月中已经创造了2 610亿美元的收益。如果胜诉,这场诉讼将允许非律师身份的投资者向律师事务所注入资金——首先以纽约、新泽西和康涅狄格第三个州作为初期目的开始试点,而后可能拓展到美国其他地区。除了哥伦比亚特区以外,当前美国的律师事务所只能采取单一的公司形式,即只能由律师投资组建合营企业。无论是势单力薄的事务所,还是像美国众达律师事务所(全美最大的律师事务所,共拥有2 400多名律师和800个合伙人)这样的龙头企业,无不例外。

关于这个案子一直争论不休,其中带有利己主义色彩。雅各比·迈尔斯公司声称现有法规侵犯了其自由言论和结社的权利。一旦新规定允许,非律师身份的投资者们将纷纷购买大量的公司股权,并坐享厚利。公司常务董事安德鲁·芬克斯坦认为,外部资金能够促进技术升级,并充分利用规模效益。此举的目的是让更多的低收入客户享受公平与正义。考虑到可能有人会反对这一想法,他说这些话的时候带着愤愤不平的口吻。

同样可以预见的是,美国律师协会反对诉讼案可能带来的变革。他们制定了相关条例,将间接约束律师行为(美国各州将条例的执行权委托给各地法院,而法院通常要遵循美国律师协会的"范式规定")。该协会认为,律师不是商人,没有责任维护损益底线;相反,他们是专业人士,承担着道德义务,必须最大程度地保障客户的利益。业外投资者可能迫使律师受理垃圾诉讼案或者仓促处理案件以确保实现利益的最大化。

但时下美国不争的现实证明变革是亟须的。许多律师事务所的综合实力不及其各分公司的总和。合作方是半独立的大牌公司,招募非合伙律师为其效力。几乎所有的工作都按小时计费,这意味着高效率反而会影响收入。相反,一家拥有专业经理人和现代电脑系统的综合性公司可以开发出供重复使用的工作流程。一些小公司开始努力尝试现代化的公司运营模式。它们以快捷优质的服务及合理公正的收费赢得客户的青睐。允许业外投资将有助于促使此类公司不断增加并扩大其经营规模。

Ⅲ. 参考译文:

Safeguard the Law and Order for Business Development

The project of the Guangdong-Hong Kong-Macao Greater Bay Area is the national strategy devised, deployed and promoted by General Secretary Xi Jinping. In March 2020, the Supreme People's Procuratorate issued the *Guidelines of Fully Exercising Procuratorial Functions for the Development of the Guangdong-Hong Kong-Macao Greater Bay Area*, requiring procuratorial organs to fully exercise procuratorial functions, and to provide highly efficient legal services and judicial guarantees for the development of the Greater Bay Area.

Guangdong's procuratorial organs have been taking further actions to renovate judicial concept, deepen reform and innovation, develop a global vision, give full play to various procuratorial functions, explore cooperation mechanism of judicial exchanges so as to facilitate the construction of the Greater Bay Area with quality judicial and procuratorial services.

The development of a first-class bay area requires a top-grade legalized setting for business development. Upholding and adhering to the concept of "superb business environment based on the rule of law", Guangdong's procuratorial organs start with actions on serving and ensuring the sound development of the private economy and remain committed to the equal and comprehensive protection principle, providing friendly, comfortable and healthy business environment for all kinds of market players. In order to ensure effective and efficient judicial guarantees for the enterprise development in the Greater Bay Area, the procuratorial organs also actively participate in the normalization and regulation of the market economic order, and punish criminal acts that hinder the personal and property rights of private enterprises and entrepreneurs according to the law.

Legal supervision over cases related to enterprises has been intensified, focusing on supervising and redressing the problems of not filing cases that should be on file, filing cases illegally and using criminal means to intervene in economic disputes. Special attention has been paid to supervising and redressing the trial and enforcement activities related to the economic disputes of private enterprises, as well taking the lead in issuing guidance on intensifying the legal supervision on civil litigation fraud.

In order to meet the judicial needs for the development of market economy, the communication channel between enterprises and procuratorates has been kept open by means of convening forums, organizing procuratorial open days and popularizing laws into enterprises. In this way, Guangdong's procuratorates may have an in-depth understanding of the judicial needs of the enterprises in the Greater Bay Area, provide enterprises with more intimately customized and precisely selected legal services, and encourage more social communities to do a contribution to the innovation and entrepreneurship in this area.

Ⅳ. 1. constitution   2. civil law   3. administrative law   4. criminal law
   5. 反不正当竞争法   6. 证券法   7. 土地管理法   8. 审计法

Ⅴ. 1. B 2. A 3. B 4. A 5. A 6. B 7. A 8. A

Ⅵ.

Construction of China's Legal System of Personal Housing Property Tax

Abstract: Personal housing property tax can raise the holding costs of houses, curb the speculation of housing directly, and play an important role in curbing high housing prices. Personal housing property tax can also provide stable local financial resources and secure fair distribution of social wealth. China should construct a legal system of personal housing property tax, coordinate the relationship between personal housing property tax and land transfer fund, establish the real estate tax system of "high maintainance, low flowing", and enact unified *Property Tax Law*. China should also establish a unified registration system of real estate, and improve the legal system of property assessment in order to pave the way for comprehensively implementing personal housing property tax.

Keywords: high housing prices; personal housing property tax; legal system

Ⅶ.（略）

Ⅷ.

英译汉练习：
1. 圣诞节对于我们所有人都有其引人之处，那就是温暖、爱恋、关怀、团结、融洽和奉献。
2. 我们还录制了如何申请签证的信息。您可以拨打使馆电话收听申请指南。
3. 众所周知，由于猫的眼睛比人类的眼睛能吸收更多光线，所以猫在黑夜也能看得非常清楚。
4. 我不认为无论做什么，我们的命运都一样；但是我确实相信如果什么都不做，我们的命运将是一样的。

汉译英练习：
1. **It is** our complicated human brain **that** makes possible all types of complicated mental activities.
2. **It doesn't alter the fact that** he is the man responsible for the delay of the meeting.
3. Discipline **is given much less emphasis than** self-discipline in troops.
4. The revolt **spread more furiously throughout the country**, despite the fact they they had tried in vain to stamp it out.

Chapter 5 Cultural & Creative Design 文创设计

Ⅰ.（略）

Ⅱ. 参考译文：

永恒的芭比娃娃

芭比娃娃是全世界最有名的玩偶。谁不认识她呀？她的真名叫芭芭拉·米利森特·罗伯茨。1959年3月9日，芭比娃娃在纽约玩具展上第一次与公众见面。美泰玩具公司的联合创始人露丝·汉德勒和丈夫埃利奥特·汉德勒共同设计了这款娃娃。

上世纪 50 年代，露丝发现与那些看起来很孩子气的娃娃相比，女儿更喜欢玩长相成人化的娃娃，常常会花上好几个小时给可分拆的娃娃反复更换服饰。当时，市面上绝大多数娃娃都是按照儿童的长相设计的。露丝意识到自己心目中的商业理念，主张设计一款青春靓丽的洋娃娃。然而，她的丈夫兼商业伙伴并不认同这个想法。

在一次欧洲之旅中，夫妻俩发现了一款很受欢迎的荷兰娃娃，名叫莉莉。这是一个受成人卡通启发设计而成的娃娃。美泰公司出资购买莉莉的版权并停止生产这款娃娃，开始着手生产露丝心目中的洋娃娃。他们设想给女孩儿们提供一种全新的娃娃，以适应女性开始尝试的各种社会变化，从而使得女孩儿们可以对娃娃产生认同感。他们给娃娃取名芭比，以纪念汉德勒夫妇的女儿芭芭拉。这款娃娃首次亮相玩具博览会就轰动了市场。面对大批订单，公司一度甚至为此抓狂，订单应接不暇，娃娃供不应求！

第一款芭比娃娃一头金发，非常时尚，穿着斑马纹泳衣。很快，芭比就有了新的伙伴。几年以来，美泰公司设计了更多的娃娃走进芭比的生活。除了众多朋友，芭比还多了几个妹妹。最著名的是凯利、切尔西和斯泰西，她们都在 10 到 13 岁之间。同时芭比的身边还多了一位永恒的男朋友肯尼。男性版的芭比娃娃以汉德勒夫妇的儿子肯尼斯的名字命名。

从少女模特出道，芭比拥有了很多不同的职业。她当过牙医、体操运动员、老师、舞蹈演员、摄影师、兽医、医生、歌手、宇航员、空姐、总统、飞行员等……是的，她有飞行员执照，而且能驾驶商用飞机。她很喜欢动物，养了 40 多只宠物，例如狗、马、猫、鹦鹉……

在每一个芭比身后，都有一个由 500 名专业人士组成的团队奋战在洛杉矶美泰研发中心。在芭比娃娃的制作过程中，技术和设计至关重要，团队成员实现了最新技术与传统方法的完美结合。芭比娃娃的制造过程纷繁复杂。娃娃的身体由注塑成型系统制作而成，面部手绘而成，头发则由缝纫机固定。头部固定在身体上之后，就需要理发、设计发型。芭比的衣服也是手工缝制的。美泰公司的设计师们观看全球最主流的 T 台秀，紧跟每季服装款式的潮流。

正如我们的社会经历各种变迁，这些年来芭比的形象也不断演变。最初，芭比的身材比例失真，面部表情也过于严肃和老气。为了适应新时代的潮流，娃娃身体各部件之间更加灵活，身材也发生了变化。现在芭比的腰围变粗了，胸围变小了，呈现更自然放松的姿势。为了让更多的小女孩对娃娃产生认同感，2016 年，美泰公司推出了一款新的玩偶系列，轰动了半个世界。时尚芭比娃娃出现了，她们身体各部分的尺寸和比例更加逼真，包括不同身材、肤色、眼睛颜色和发型等。

芭比娃娃是历史上销量最大的娃娃，美泰公司也一跃成为世界上最有价值的 20 个品牌之一，在玩具界更是名列榜首。该公司已经在 140 多个国家开展营销业务，据估计每分钟就能成功售出两个芭比娃娃。收集玩具是一种非常流行的爱好，尤其是收集芭比娃娃。每年都有超过 100 种不同型号的芭比娃娃诞生，包括芭比的家人和朋友。此外，公司还推出不少价格不菲的特别版芭比。

50多年的发展史成就了芭比之梦,这一切对于玩具娃娃来说几乎令人难以置信。芭比娃娃不仅是一个玩偶,她更是一种时尚和社交的标志。芭比的人气一路飙升,人们对芭比的痴迷似乎永无止境!

Ⅲ. 参考译文:

Cultural Factors in Designing

The U.S. Postal Service has recently issued a new stamp to commemorate the 2008 Olympic Games in Beijing. It was designed by a Chinese-American graphic artist from Hawaii. The artist himself may not be a household name, but his stamps are recognized around the world.

It is just before noon, and business is bustling at this Honolulu Post Office. Jane Yee is buying a sheet of Olympic Games stamps. "I do like the stamps very much. They are terrific! The colors are beautiful and it shows the gymnasts in action." she says. She is also pleased to discover that Clarence Lee, one of Hawaii's best-known graphic designers, created this stamp. The stamp depicts a leaping gymnast in bright red, which, according to Lee, honors the spirit of the Games. "It is just so energetic and appealing, and it's very athletic in motion."

This is not the first time Lee designs a stamp. In 1992, the U.S. Postal Service asked Lee to design a New Year stamp to honor Chinese Americans. Looking ahead to the Year of the Rooster, Lee already had a clear idea of what he wanted. His rooster stamp was very popular, not just in the U.S., but also in China, bringing in more than $5 million in sales. Obviously, the U.S. Postal Service had never expected that there are some 20 million stamp collectors in China. Take into account the fact that this was the first U.S. stamp characterized by a Chinese character, Chinese paper cut artwork and Chinese-style boldness of using colors, and the promotion was very successful, the stamps were sold up very soon. Because the rooster stamp had been such a big hit, the Postal Service commissioned Lee to design a set of stamps focusing on the theme of the 12 Chinese Zodiac symbols. As Lee once mentioned, the stamp of the Pig was his favorite, on which a little pig is just flying through the air, very delighted and lively.

Today, Lee is internationally recognized for his stamp designs, which often incorporate a sense of cultural awareness. He has created eye-catching logos for major companies in Hawaii and around the world, as well as posters and brochures for special events. In 1994, Lee designed America's first joint-issue stamp with China. The two-stamp set featured a black-necked crane and a whooping crane. When asked what stamp he would design today if he could pick any theme, Lee answered without hesitation. "I think it would be world peace."

Now in his 70s, Clarence Lee continues to design and create art. He is still amazed that his smallest projects — stamps — have become his biggest claim to fame.

Ⅳ. 1. 文化视觉化　　　2. 设计美学　　　3. 设计原理　　　4. 设计批评
　　5. 感性艺术加工　　6. design culture　　7. formal aesthetics
　　8. visual identity　　9. procedure of product design

Ⅴ. 1. B　2. A　3. A　4. A　5. A　6. B　7. B　8. A

Ⅵ.

On Exploitation of Cultural & Creative Design in Ethnic Minority Areas

Abstract: The ethnic minorities in the Nenjiang River Basin in China have been living in remote areas for a long time, which makes it inconvenient for them to communicate with the outside world. As a result, these nationalities have developed and passed down a unique, natural, simple and unsophisticated culture. This project studies the traditional materials (such as the skin, horn, hair and teeth of animals such as cattle, sheep, deer, horse and fish, and the stalk, root, skin of plants such as elm, pine, birch, poplar and willow), processing skills and technological innovation of two representative nationalities, namely Daur Nationality and Manchu Nationality. In this way, it helps us better understand and inherit the feat of cultural design, providing sources of insight and inspiration for designing modern cultural and creative products.

Keywords: Daur Nationality; Manchu Nationality; cultural & creative products; design

Ⅶ.（略）

Ⅷ.
英译汉练习：

1. 过度加热会破坏维生素 C。

2. Y 射线不受电场影响。

3. 众所周知，世界是由物质构成的。

4. 英语正在**遭到**一种"官腔语言的致命病毒"的**侵害**,这种病毒已经感染了许多政治家的谈吐和思想,其中包括托尼·布莱尔和乔治·布什。

汉译英练习:

1. This affair must **be dealt with** at the appropriate time with appropriate means.
2. National Day **is celebrated** with great joy and excitement on Oct. 1 **by** the Chinese people of all nationalities every year.
3. The visiting guests **were escorted to** the Yellow Crane Tower last Sunday.
4. He **had been totally asked** ten questions during the interview, and all the interviewers **were greatly impressed** by his excellent performance.

Chapter 6　Biochemical Engineering 生化工程

Ⅰ.(略)

Ⅱ. 参考译文:

化学武器:沙林毒气

沙林是一种快速起效的人造神经剧毒剂。最初于1938年研制于德国,主要用作杀虫剂。不过,据美国疾病预防控制中心(CDC)称,沙林的功效远远超过普通杀虫剂。沙林可溶于水和食物,从而使人中毒,或者以气态释放,进而对更大范围的人群造成更为严重的伤害。

通常,受害者吸入毒气却一无所知。沙林是一种无色无味的液体,它的挥发速度基本上和水分蒸发的速度相同,因而是一种易挥发的神经毒剂。在1988年的哈莱卜杰大屠杀中,伊拉克前总统萨达姆下令在库尔德市释放沙林毒气,三天内造成至少5 000平民死亡。1995年,东京的一场地铁恐怖袭击同样使用了沙林毒气,致使13人丧生。易挥发性意味着通常须在使用前夕才开始配制沙林,而且一旦配制完成,需要以液态储存。沙林还具有强腐蚀性,需储存于特制容器,以防泄漏。

吸入沙林毒气几秒钟之内,受害者开始出现眼睛疼、流口水、虚弱、呕吐、腹泻、心率失常等症状。受害者的衣物将持续释放毒气长达30分钟之久,致使周边更多的人相继中毒。对于液态沙林而言,受害者在中毒后几分钟至18小时内的任何时候都有可能出现病症。如果摄入大量液态或气态沙林,中毒者会出现更为严重和更加痛苦的症状,比如抽搐、麻痹、丧失呼吸功能,甚至死亡。

如果仅接触少量沙林,大部分人都能恢复健康。卫生部门建议,如果在室内摄入沙林,最好转移到户外,以便气体散发,减少毒气吸入量。尽快把接触毒气的衣物脱掉,用肥皂和清水冲洗接触毒素的部位,从而减少重症危害。美国疾病预防控制中心证实,如果及时将受害者送往医院接受解毒治疗,他们就能够幸免于难,避免出现长达一周或半个月的神经异常现象。然而,如果大量接触沙林而没有得到医治,很可能会导致受害者死亡。所以说,沙林是一种强效的神经毒剂。

Ⅲ. 参考译文:

Crude Fractionation

Distillation is an operation by which a mixture of mutually soluble liquids is physically separated into fractions, or cuts, according to their boiling points (or, rather, ranges). At this step, the feedstock is raised to a boiling point and partly vaporizes — this produces an overhead product and a bottom product, both differing from the feedstock in composition. At existing petroleum refineries, this is done in stills in a single pass. As a result, the low-boiling fractions passing into the vapour phase remain in the still and bring down the partial pressure of the vaporizing high-boiling fractions. Because of this, the operation may be carried out at a lower temperature.

The single-pass evaporation followed by vapor condensation produces a light fraction and a heavy fraction. The light fraction is higher and the heavy fraction is lower in the low-boiling constituents than the feed. In other words, one fraction is enriched with low-boiling components and the other fraction with high-boiling components. However, this operation fails to fractionate the crude to the desired degree and to yield the products that boil with the specified temperature ranges. For this reason, it is followed by rectification.

Rectification is a diffusion operation which has as its objective to separate liquids according to their boiling points by causing the vapour and the liquid to come in contact countercurrent repeatedly.

Crude fractionation systems may be single-stage or double-stage, with the required heat supplied by direct-fired furnace-type tubular heater, also called pipe (or tube) still. Furthermore, they may operate at atmospheric pressure or under a vacuum, depending on the overall plant layout and the quality of the crudes coming in for refining. Sometimes, a crude fractionation system may combine operation at atmospheric pressure, known as atmospheric distillation, and that under a vacuum, known as vacuum flashing.

Ⅳ. 1. coloring/pigment addictive   2. mineral additive   3. nutritional additive
     4. flavour additive   5. 酸化剂   6. 乳化剂

7. 防腐剂　　　　　　　　8. 抗氧化剂

Ⅴ. 1. A　2. B　3. B　4. A　5. A　6. B　7. A　8. B

Ⅵ.

Map-based Cloning for Plants Gene Isolation

Abstract: Traditional gene cloning methods by functional and phonetypical analyses have some disadvantages, including unknown products expressed by relation genes and uneasy-operation to the gene. The technique of map-based cloning has been perfected now, and already become a kind of valuable method for gene isolation. It has been extensively applied in a lot of plant gene cloning. This paper briefly introduces the principle of map-based cloning, and gives detailed description of the operation steps by map-based cloning: screening molecular marker connected with target gene, orientating target gene, constructing big fragment genome library as well as screening and identifying the target gene. This paper also summarizes the progress of map-based cloning on plant gene isolation, and sets forward the prospect on application of map-based cloning. In the future, with the guidance of genomic heredity system theory and at the backgrounds of molecular marker in high pleomorphism, the application of map-based cloning might achieve more shining progress in plant gene cloning.

Keywords: map-based cloning; molecular markers; mapping; chromosome walking

Ⅶ. (略)

Ⅷ.　1. ABCD　2. ABCD　3. A

Chapter 7　Electronic Technology　电子技术

Ⅰ. (略)

Ⅱ. 参考译文：

人 工 智 能

20世纪50年代正值数字计算机问世不久，人们便开始围绕"机器能否思考"这一问题开展严谨的猜想。1947年设计成功的一部机器能够独立参与国际象棋比赛,这就向一些著名的计算机科学家证实了机器具有演绎推理能力。这些科学家认为由于"自然的"机器——人类——能够思考,因此"人造的"机器也可以具备思考能力。然而,另一些科学家则认为计算机永远不可能复制人类的思维能力。自此,人工智能就成了顶尖高校不断探索和争论的课题。

20世纪70年代后期,专家系统开始逐步兴起。人们认为该系统是至今为止人工智能研究领域最具实用价值的应用开发。

一台具有人工智能的计算机会运用常识、判断力和本能完成逻辑推理,而这些能力至今为止仍属于人类独有的特质。计算机科学家正在尝试研发新型的软件和计算机,从而实现机器独立决策、错误更正、解决问题、自动编程等能力。若要研发出能够复制和模仿人脑复杂结构的计算机,这项任务可谓是一个雄心勃勃的大工程。

导致人工智能研究进展缓慢的一个原因是科学家们无法就其定义达成共识。更准确地讲,这个定义似乎一直在变化,因为计算机领域具有革新价值的技术一旦实现就不足为奇了。

有人指出,当计算机首次参与西洋跳棋或国际象棋比赛,人们将其视作人工智能运用的典范。而现今,廉价袖珍型机器比当初的庞然大物表现更为出色,而人们却不再将其列入人工智能的范畴。

此外,还有其他一系列问题,例如计算机是否真正具备独立意识、自我认知和创造能力?

计算机能够模仿一部分人类思维,例如完成某些复杂任务所必须的逻辑性很强的思维过程。但是计算机具备智能吗?有些专家表示,计算机只不过是一个机械化的低能仆人,也就是在有限的领域具有卓越技能的呆板的机器。

Ⅲ. 参考译文:

Intelligent Fraud

The bot, called SNAPR, was an automated phishing system, capable of tracing the whims of specific individuals and coaxing them toward that moment when they would inadvertently download spyware onto their computers or mobile phones. "Archaeologists believe they've found the tomb of Alexander the Great is in the U.S., for the first time," the bot tweeted at one unsuspecting user.

Even with the odd grammatical misstep, SNAPR succeeded in eliciting a click as often as 66 percent of the time, on par with human hackers who craft phishing messages by hand. The bot was unarmed, merely a proof of concept. But in the wave of concern over political hacking, fake news and the dark side of social networking, it illustrated why the landscape of fakery will only darken further.

The bot built what is called a neural network, a complex mathematical system that can learn tasks by analyzing vast amounts of data. A neural network can learn to recognize a dog by gleaning patterns from thousands of dog photos. Similarly, it can learn to identify spoken language by sifting through old tech-support calls. A neural network can also learn to write phishing messages by inspecting tweets, Reddit posts, and previous online hacks.

Today, the same mathematical technique is infusing machines with a wide range of humanlike powers, from speech recognition to language translation. In many cases, this new breed of artificial intelligence is also an ideal means of deceiving large numbers of people over the Internet. Mass manipulation is about to get a whole lot easier.

Many technology observers have expressed concerns at the rise of AI that generates deepfakes — fake images that look like the real thing. What began as a way of putting anyone's head onto the shoulders of a porn star has evolved into a tool for seamlessly putting any image or audio into any video.

The threat will only expand as researchers develop systems that can metabolize and learn from increasingly large collections of data. Neural networks can generate believable sounds as well as images. This is what enables digital assistants such as Apple Siri to sound more human than they did in years past.

Ⅳ. 1. wired communications   2. wireless communications   3. 广域网   4. 城干网
    5. access network   6. CCTV (closed-circuit television)
    7. 无线局域网   8. 卫星通信

Ⅴ. 1. A   2. A   3. B   4. B   5. A   6. B   7. B   8. B

Ⅵ.

Design & Simulation of a New Wireless Network Security Communication Protocol

Abstract: Wireless network technology is an important symbol of the 21st century global IT development. With the rapid development of wireless networks, more attention has been paid to its security. Since the wireless network information is transmitted by microwave radiation, within the area covered by the wireless network nodes, all workstations are likely to receive information, which causes a great threat to the security of the information dissemination, leading to various problems related to wireless security. In order to protect the wireless security, we should continuously improve the security management mechanism to effectively prevent the security risks, and promote the healthy development of wireless network security. In this project, a simple wireless network security communication protocol is designed and simulated in the NS2 network simulation software, and the process of link connections is observed. The result of simulation enables us to learn more about the operation of the wireless network security communication protocol, which will provide a reliable basis for the analysis and design of the communication protocol.

Keywords: wireless network technology; wireless security; communication protocol

Ⅶ.（略）

Ⅷ. 1. ABC 2. B 3. C 4. C 5. D 6. ABCD 7. ABD

Chapter 8　Intelligent Manufacturing 智能制造

Ⅰ.（略）

Ⅱ. 参考译文：

制造业的革新

机器人是一种可重复编程的多功能操作器,其设计用途是通过一系列不同的程控动作输送物料、零件、工具及一些特殊装置,从而控制完成多种不同任务。以上即目前普遍认可的对机器人的定义,突出工业机器人可以重复编程且能够沿多种不同轨迹运动的两大特点。

随着工业革命的到来,制造工艺体现出高度的专业化和机械化。生产者不再独自参与设计、制造、运输等全过程,取而代之的是由工人和机器来完成这几大流程中的某个专门的任务。这些独立个体间的沟通交流是通过图纸、技术要求、任务书、工艺规程以及其他通讯辅助手段完成的。为了确保成品质量符合设计要求,人们引入了质量控制的概念。

机械化生产阶段实现了批量生产、零件互换、精度分级、规格一致等优点。其缺点则表现为因缺乏协调性和集成化而导致大量浪费。

自动化技术改善了专业化制造各环节的生产过程,增强了操作人员和机器的工作效率。例如,计算机辅助设计（CAD）增强了设计人员和制图人员的工作能力,电脑数值控制（CNC）增强了机械师和机辅规划人员的工作能力。但是自动化带来的进步仅限于各个独立的生产环节。因此,该技术尚未充分发挥其潜力。

随着计算机时代的来临,制造业似乎又回到了初始状态。最开始,制造业就是一个纯粹的集成概念,而计算机集成制造(CIM)又一次使其回到一种单一的状态。然而,现如今的制造集成化与过去手工时代的集成化存在显著差异。首先,手工时代的集成化是由人脑完成的,而现代化制造过程是由电脑实现的。其次,现代制造环境中的工艺流程体现出专业化和自动化的特点。

通过仔细观察过去几年中CIM某些生产环节所发生的变化,我们可以发现该领域取得了历史性突破。例如设计、规划以及生产等工艺流程不断发展,就连配合完成这些工艺的工具设备也华丽变身。设计已经从使用直尺、三角板、铅笔、比例尺和橡皮擦的手工过程演变成为CAD自动化过程;工艺规划已经从使用规程表、图解和图表的手工过程演变成为自动化的计算机辅助工艺规划(CAPP);而生产已经从手动控制机器的过程演变成为计算机辅助制造(CAM)的自动化流程。

Ⅲ. 参考译文:

Automation Technology

Flexible automation technology is a kind of new automation technology based on computer technology, which is automatically able for technical operations, and to fulfill the set processing goals. In today's mechanical engineering industry, this technology is needed to greatly improve the productivity, so as to promote the development of industrialization. At present, flexible automation technology has become an indispensable part in the mechanical engineering manufacturing. With mainly the numerical control technology as the core, it also combines advanced information science and technology, mechanical manufacturing technology and high-end computer equipment to develop industrial machinery manufacture.

For industrial development, the application of automation technology in the mechanical engineering shows important significance: (1) It can greatly improve production efficiency, increase the quantity of the products, and thus greatly reduce the labor intensity of workers. (2) It can reduce the production cost without hurting the quality of the products, and thus greatly increase the product benefits. These two points prove that flexible automation technology represents the developing trend of modern industrial machinery manufacturing industry.

Integrated automation technology refers to the technology which improves and specifies the manufacturing process of the mechanical engineering on the basis of the current information technology, and at the same time efficiently integrates all the relevant information and technology during the whole production process so as to enhance the integration function and develop the mechanical production. With these advantages, the technology has, so far, gained wide recognitions in the national mechanical engineering manufacture. Meanwhile, with the rapid development of the computer integrated system, the integrated automation technology finds application in many other aspects. From the perspective of today's market development, it is able to ensure the largest benefit from the research and development to the production and control.

Ⅳ. 1. front view　2. cutaway view　3. vertical view　4. assembly drawing
　　5. 零件图　　6. 布置图　　7. 尺寸标注

Ⅴ. 1. B　2. A　3. B　4. B　5. B　6. B　7. A　8. A

Ⅵ.

Origin, Development & Prospects of Intelligent Manufacturing

Abstract: This thesis introduces the background of the concept "intelligent manufacturing", its research domain and target, the co-relation between artificial intelligence and Intelligent Multimode Terminal (IMT), the material and theoretical basis of intelligent manufacturing, characteristics and framework structure of intelligent manufacturing system. Intelligent machining center (IMC), development trend of intelligent manufacturing technology as well as the research achievements and existing problems of intelligent manufacturing system are also briefly introduced.

Keywords: intelligent manufacturing; Intelligent Multimode Terminal (IMT); Intelligent Machining Center (IMC)

Ⅶ. (略)

Ⅷ. 1. B　2. ABE　3. ABCDEF　4. B　5. A

Chapter 9　Civil Engineering & Architecture 土木建筑

Ⅰ. (略)

Ⅱ. 参考译文：

透 光 水 泥

意大利建筑师们已经研制出一种"透光水泥"，可以让光线直接涌入房间，使墙体看起来如同一扇扇巨大的窗户。这种建材名为"我是光"，内含许多微型小孔，能够透射光线，却并不影响建筑结构的完整性。走近一步细看，墙体布满直径为 2 至 3 毫米的孔隙，其排列图案简直令人叹为观止。从某些角度或从远处看，墙体和普通水泥墙几乎没有任何区别。然而，在阳光灿烂的日子里，由透光水泥建成的房间所呈现出来的效果，恰好如同嵌入墙壁的一道滤光网眼，阳光透过光孔照射进来。

意大利水泥集团建筑师们在新型混合配剂中加入特殊树脂，制成这种透光水泥。迄今为止，上海世博会意大利馆是全球唯一的一座透光水泥建筑。而且早就有人指出，这种透光建筑可以节约白昼照明所需的用电量。

意大利世博展馆高 18 米，其中 40% 的墙体采用的是"我是光"新型材料，或者说共使用了由 189 吨透光水泥制成的 3 774 块透明和半透明水泥板。每块透明水泥板约含 50 个小孔，可以达到 20% 左右的透明度。半透明水泥板的透明度约为 10%，通过调节混合配剂中的树脂含量制成。

之前类似的尝试是在混凝土中加入光纤，但意大利水泥公司认为使用树脂的效果更好。塑料树脂比光纤便宜得多，因而生产"透光水泥"的成本就低。此外，树脂的视角比光纤更广，所以透光水泥对光线的"捕捉"能力也就更强。这一特性实际上增加了建材的透光性能，同时也改善了建筑物的采光效果。公司之所以接受建设意大利馆的挑战，正是因为他们希望能从中找到一种"创新高效的节能方法"。公司以每天 200 块的速度制造出 3774 块透光水泥板用于意大利馆的建设。目前，透光水泥已经申请了专利保护，而意大利水泥集团尚未决定是否在全球范围内予以推广应用。

Ⅲ. 参考译文：

Building Structure

A structure is the part of a building that carries its weight. A structure may be a dwelling house, or a pyramid in Egypt, or a dam on a river. A building is a structure with a roof and much of civil engineering structural design is the design of building structure. The part of the building that holds up the weight and load is called the structural part. Parts such as windows that do not hold up the building are the non-structural parts. Building structures are classified into many forms according to different materials, such as concrete structure, steel structure and masonry structure.

In reinforced concrete structures, steel reinforcing bars are embedded in concrete structures where tensile stress may occur to make the good compressive strength of concrete structures fully put into action. Generally speaking, reinforced concrete structures possess the following features such as large dead mass, high stiffness, good durability, long curing period, being easily cracked and so on. Reinforced concrete systems are composed of a variety of concrete structural elements that, when synthesized in a certain way, produce a total system. The components can be broadly classified into floor slabs, beams, columns, walls and foundations.

Steel structure refers to a widely applied building structures in which steel plays the leading role. Steel offers much better compression and tension than concrete and enables lighter construction. Steel structures use three-dimensional trusses, so they can achieve a larger span than reinforced concrete counterparts.

The earliest use of masonry can be traced back to two thousand years ago in China. Before the use of reinforced concrete, masonry such as stones, bricks as well as wood were the main construction materials. Even in the modern time, due to its good quality of heat preservation and easy construction, most countries especially the developing ones still use masonry as the major material for civil buildings. The masonry structure takes its leading role in the developing countries for its lower cost. But as is known to all, masonry materials such as bricks or blocks are a type of brittle materials with strong compressive capacity but weak tensile capacity, which often suffer from relatively poor deformability or ductility. Buildings built by ductile materials can endure severe earthquakes and would not fall down even when they are seriously damaged, but those built by brittle materials would suddenly fall down once the earthquake load exceeds their structural resistant capacity. Thus, strict limitations on the construction of masonry houses have to be specified to those areas where they may encounter severe earthquakes.

Ⅳ. 1. lime   2. timber   3. asbestos
    4. mortar   5. facing and plastering material
    6. 防腐蚀材料   7. 双层玻璃   8. 防火材料

Ⅴ. 1. B   2. B   3. A   4. A   5. B   6. A   7. B   8. B

Ⅵ.

An Experimental Study on Relations among Permeability, Strain and Bedding of Soft Rock

Abstract: In civil engineering, hydraulic engineering and nuclear wastes disposal engineering, increasing attention is being focused on the influence of stress state on rock permeability. The permeability coefficients of two typical soft rocks, i.e., clayey siltstone and brown mudstone, have been investigated by the transient pulse technique in the complete stress-strain curve. The results show that: ① The permeability coefficient of clayey siltstone decreases in the stage of elastic deformation but increases in the stage of plastic deformation and the fractured phases. The permeability coefficient on the direction vertical to the bedding plane is larger than that on the direction parallel to the bedding plane; ② The permeability of brown mudstone decreases in the stage of plastic deformation but keeps stable in the stage of creep deformation. The permeability coefficient on the direction vertical to the bedding plane is similar to that on the direction parallel to the bedding plane. Combined with the stress-train curves, it can be deduced that in the stage of elastic deformation, the permeability coefficient of clayey siltstone is mainly influenced by porosity and small cracks; and in the stage of plastic deformation and the fractured phases, it is mainly influenced by small crack. In the complete deformation process, the permeability coefficient of brown mudstone is influenced by porosity and small cracks, both effects are not distinguishable.

Keywords: rock mechanics; soft rock; complete stress-strain curve; permeability coefficient; bedding plane; experimental study

Ⅶ.（略）

Ⅷ. 1. ABCD 2. ACD 3. ABDFHI 4. BDEFILMNO 5. ABE

Chapter 10　Perfume & Aroma　香精香料

Ⅰ.（略）

Ⅱ. 参考译文：

法国香水

说到香水艺术,没有哪个国家可以与法国媲美。香奈儿、克里斯汀·迪奥或雅诗兰黛等许多香水行业的知名品牌都是法国货。就国际香水销售而言,法国无疑独占鳌头,占据了30%的全球市场份额。法国旗舰公司路易威登集团是全世界最大的奢侈品公司,旗下生产的法国香水和化妆品在公司最知名的品牌系列中脱颖而出。

如今,虽然香水业的大牌都设在巴黎,而且"巴黎香水"备受青睐,但法国香水业真正的核心区域其实是位于尼斯西北部的格拉斯小镇。格拉斯距离海岸约20公里,海拔350米,属于温和的地中海气候,特别适合园艺,尤其适合种植茉莉花。茉莉花是香水行业最重要的天然香料之一。当然,格拉斯也以生产其他多种天然香料而闻名,包括薰衣草、桃金娘、玫瑰和含羞草等。

格拉斯的香水行业涉及约60家不同的公司,雇佣员工人数近3 500人。尽管格拉斯不得不与时俱进,在生产天然香料的同时也生成合成香料,但格拉斯仍然作为天然香料产地而享有盛誉。非凡的香水制作工艺包括提取花香,并将其制成各种可转化成香水的浓缩原料,最终将其转化生成香水装在小瓶中出售,价格不菲。从鲜花中提取香味的传统方法有浸渍法(将鲜花浸泡在可吸收其香味的液体中)或蒸馏法。由此产生的浓缩液称为"精油",人们通过混合调配这些精油制造香水。

近年来,尤其是在低端香水市场,从花卉和其他植物中提取的天然香料已在很大程度上被化学合成的香料所取代,因而人们可以在世界任何地方批量生产合成香料。但是,在使用天然植物萃取精华生产顶级高品质香水的过程中,法国香水大师们所掌握的高超技艺仍无可替代。在地中海阳光的普照下,格拉斯地区香水制作的秘诀和工艺代代相传,其精髓是其他地区无法复制或效仿的。尽管法国香水行业利润超级丰厚,但迄今为止,其他国家发现根本无法挑战法国作为世界优质香水供应商的声誉。

Ⅲ. 参考译文:

Development of Scents and Perfumes

It has been a long history since scents and perfumes were first utilized. Its development differs from country to country, which has been closely connected to a nation's cultural customs and living habits. In antiquity, the ancient Greeks and Romans were keen users of scents. Indeed, the art of perfumery can be traced right back to the origins of western civilization in Mesopotamia. Scents and perfumes were used to cover bad body odors, and make people smell attractive instead. That was a very important common activity in times of bathing.

The history of the use of scents and perfumes by ancient Egyptians can be traced back to about 3500 BC, much earlier than any other civilization. Ancient Egyptians learnt how to make perfume and moisturizing ointment by soaking the scents with oil, filtering the liquid with cloth or rubbing the petals into fat to absorb and preserve their fragrance. The earliest perfume created by humans was the "Kyphi", which was invented by the Egyptians. However, since the method of refining high purity alcohol was not grasped at that time, it should be more accurately called "fragrant oil", which was specially made by priests and Pharaohs. The use of perfumes became increasingly preralent in ancient Egypt in 1500 BC. Perfume essence and ointments were commonly used in and after bathing. They were usually stored in beautifully designed containers, which have been soundly proved by the funeral objects from ancient tombs excavated in modern times. It even became illegal at that time for Egyptians to appear in public places without wearing perfume. After people died, Egyptians wrapped the bodies with scents to become mummies. They believed that the corrosion resistance of scents would make their souls immortal.

Ancient Greece deified perfume, believing that perfume was the invention of the gods and the smell of fragrance meant the arrival and blessing of gods. Women must wear perfume at religious ceremonies. In ancient Greece, women who produced perfume learned from the crafts and methods adopted by ancient Egyptians as well as brought some improvements.

A great advance in perfume history took place in the early Middle Ages, when Arabs invented large-scale plant distillation. In the twelfth century, the Arabian discovered that perfume essence dissolved by alcohol could release fragrance slowly, and a number of concentrated essence had also been better preserved by alcohol.

Ⅳ. 1. aftershave / shaving lotion   2. <2%   3. 古龙水   4. 1~2 hours
   5. fragrance   6. 80%~85%   7. 淡香精;浓香水   8. five hours
   9. perfume   10. 20%~30%

Ⅴ. 1. A 2. B 3. B 4. A 5. B 6. A 7. B 8. B

Ⅵ.

A New Process to Manufacture Vanillin by Microbio-transformation

Abstract: Vanillin is one of the most widely-applied flavors. In this research, vanillin is manufactured by microbio-transformation with ferulic acid as substrate. Factors such as different nitrogen sources, feeding amounts and feeding approaches etc., are observed to study the effect of biocatalyst on the transformation rate of ferulic acid. The data under the experimental condition of 50L fermentators show that the final concentration of vanillin can be up to 15 g/L, with matches advanced international standard.

Keywords: microbio-transformation; vanillin; ferulic acid

Ⅶ.（略）

Ⅷ. 1. ACEF 2. A 3. B 4. B

附录1　全国大学英语四级考试翻译题型指南及真题演练

参考译文：

1. The Chinese knot is originally invented by the handicraftsmen. After innovation and improvement for hundreds of years, it has evolved into an elegant and colorful art and craft. In ancient times, it was used for recording events, while now it mainly serves a decorative purpose. The word "knot" means love, marriage and reunion in Chinese. The Chinese knot is often used as a gift to express good wishes or a talisman to ward off evil spirits. This from of handcraft has passed on for generations and become more and more popular both in China and around the world.

2. The full name of a Han Chinese consists of a family name and a given name. A distinctive feature of the Chinese name is that the family name always comes first, followed by the given name. For thousands of years, Chinese family names have been passed down through the father. Nowadays, however, it is not uncommon for a child to adopt the mother's family name. Generally, a given name is made up of one or two characters, usually carrying the parents' wishes for their child. It can be inferred from the name what kind of person the parents want their child to be, or what kind of life they expect him or her to lead. Chinese parents attach great importance to the choice of children's names, as names tend to accompany the children for their entire life.

3. The family values in China are related to its cultural traditions. Harmonious extended families used to be very admirable. It used to be quite common in the past for four generations of a family to live under the same roof. According to this tradition, many young people continued to live with their parents after marriage. Today, that tradition is under changes. As housing conditions improve, more and more young couples opt to live apart from their parents. But the connections between them still

remain strong. Many elderly people still offer help to look after their grandchildren. And young couples often take time to visit their parents, especially during important festivals such as the Spring Festival and the Mid-Autumn Festival.

4. Chinese families attach great importance to their children's education. Many parents hold that they should work hard to ensure their children's access to good education. They are not only perfectly willing to invest in their children's education, but also spend much time encouraging them to study. Most parents expect their children to get admitted to elite universities. Owing to China's adoption of reform and opening-up policy, an increasing number of parents are able to send their children to study abroad or participate in international exchange programs to broaden their horizons. Through these efforts, they expect their children grow up strong and healthy and make a contribution to the nation's development and prosperity.

5. Paper cutting is a unique form of Chinese folk art and has a history of more than 2,000 years. Paper cutting probably originates in the Han Dynasty, following the invention of paper. Since then, it has gained popularity in many places of China. The materials and tools used for paper cutting are simple: paper and scissors. Paper-cuts are usually made of red paper, because red is associated with happiness in traditional Chinese culture. Therefore, on festive occasions such as weddings and the Chinese New Year, red paper-cuts are the first choice for decorating doors and windows.

6. The mobile payment market has thrived in China during the past few years. With the advent of the mobile Internet, mobile shopping has gradually become a trend. Young people aged from 18 to 30 have constituted the largest group of the mobile payment market. Because it is quite easy to make a payment by phone, many consumers would rather pay by mobile phone than in cash or by credit card. In order to encourage people to spend more, many stores offer discounts to consumers who use the mobile payment. As is predicted by experts, the mobile payment market in China still has great potential for development in the future.

7. Lanterns originated in the Eastern Han Dynasty, and were used primarily for lighting at the beginning. In the Tang Dynasty, people used red lanterns to celebrate a stable life. Since then, lanterns have become popular in many parts of China. Lanterns are usually made of brightly-colored tissue paper in a variety of shapes and sizes. In

traditional Chinese culture, red lanterns symbolize a happy life and flourishing business, usually hung during festivals like the Spring Festival, the Lantern Festival and the National Day. Today, red lanterns can be seen in many other parts of the world.

8. Because of the rapid development of communication network, the number of smartphone users in China has increased at an astonishing rate in recent years, which has significantly changed the way many people read. Nowadays they often read news and articles on smartphones instead of buying traditional newspapers and periodicals. The development of numerous mobile apps has enabled people to read novels and other forms of literary works on their mobile phones. Therefore, the sales of paper books have been affected. But surveys show that though smartphone reading market has grown steadily, over half of the adults still enjoy reading paper books.

9. Mount Hua is located in Huayin City (Shaanxi, China), 120 kilometers away from Xi'an. It is part of the Qin Mountains, which divide not only northern and southern Shaanxi, but also south and north China. Unlike Mount Tai that used to be frequented by pilgrims, Mount Hua was not well visited as the roads up the mountain were extremely dangerous. Back then, however, those who wished to enjoy longevity ventured in Mount Hua quite a lot because numerous herbs, rare ones in particular, grew in the mountain. Since cable cars were installed in Mount Hua in the 1990s, the number of visitors has increased dramatically.

10. According to the Chinese culture, the color of red usually stands for good luck, longevity and happiness. Red can be found everywhere during Chinese Spring Festival and other joyous occasions. Money sent to family members or close friends as gifts is usually wrapped up in red envelopes. Its popularity can also be attributed to the fact that people associate the color of red with the Chinese revolution and the Communist Party of China. However, red does not always equal to good luck and joy in that the name of the dead used to be written in red. As a result, to write the names of Chinese people in red ink has been regarded as an offense.

附录2　全国大学英语六级考试翻译题型指南及真题演练

参考译文：

1. China attaches increasing importance to public libraries and encourages people to

make full use of them. The newly released statistics indicate that the number of public libraries in China is on the increase year by year. Many libraries have created a quieter and more comfortable environment for readers through renovation and expansion. Not only do large-scale public libraries provide a wide range of reference materials, but they also regularly hold lectures, exhibitions and other activities. In recent years, there have also been many digital libraries, saving the space needed to store books. In addition, some libraries have introduced self-service systems, which make it more convenient for readers to borrow and return books, and further meet the needs of readers.

2. Dongting Lake is a large, shallow lake in northeastern Hunan province, China. It is a flood basin of the Yangtze River. Hence, the lake's size largely depends on the season. The provinces of Hubei and Hunan are named after their location relative to the lake. Hubei means "North of the Lake" and Hunan, "South of the Lake". Dongting Lake is famous in Chinese culture as the birthplace of dragon boat racing, which is said to have begun on the eastern shores of Dongting Lake as a search for the body of Qu Yuan, the Chu poet and a respected patriot. Together with the lake and its surrounding attractive sceneries, the racing appeals to thousands of tourists from other parts of China and the whole world each year.

3. In the past, owning a private car was a luxury for most Chinese. Nowadays, private cars can be seen everywhere in China. Cars have become an integral part of people's life. They not only drive to and from work, but also travel around by car. The upsurging car ownership have resulted in more prevalent traffic gridlock and inadequate parking space in some cities, which has prompted local governments to introduce new rules to rein in the number of cars on the road. As air pollution gets more serious, now more and more people choose to buy new energy vehicles. The Chinese government has taken some measures to support the development of new energy vehicles.

4. China now has the largest and fastest high-speed rail network in the world. The speed of the CRH (China Railway High-Speed) train will continue to increase and more cities will build high-speed rail stations. The CRH train has greatly reduced people's travel time. Compared with the airplane, the outstanding advantage of the CRH train is punctuality, because it is basically not affected by weather or traffic control. It has transformed the way people live and become the favorite option for business travelers

today. More and more people also travel by CRH train during holidays. Many young people choose to work in one city but live in a nearby one since they can commute by CRH train every day.

5. The plum blossom, the queen of China's top ten famous flowers, originated in southern China and has been cultivated for over 3,000 years. In the depths of winter, colorful plum blossoms bloom vibrantly amidst the wind and snow, unhindered by severe frost. The plum blossom, a symbol of strength, purity and elegance in traditional Chinese culture, motivates people to break hardships and forge ahead. Since ancient times, many poets and painters have been drawing inspirations from plum blossoms and created countless immortal works. Plum blossoms are also very popular with the general public and often used as home decoration during the Spring Festival. Nanjing has designated the plum blossom as the city flower and holds the Plum Blossom Festival each year, which attracts thousands of people to Plum Blossom Hill to enjoy the full bloom in the snow irrespective of the severe cold.

6. The peony, boasting bright colors and an elegant appearance, is a symbol of peace and prosperity and thus recognized as "king of the flowers" in China. Peonies are bred and grown in many parts of the country. Over the centuries, numerous poems and paintings have been created to praise the flower. Peonies were particularly popular during the Tang Dynasty, when they were extensively cultivated in the imperial gardens and praised as the national flower. In the tenth century, the ancient city of Luoyang became the center for peony cultivation, a position it still holds today. Nowadays, thousands of tourists from home and abroad flock to Luoyang for the annual Peony Festival to both admire the unique beauty of the city's peonies and explore the history of the ancient capital of nine dynasties.

7. Chinese idioms, mostly composed of four Chinese characters, are a unique way of expression in Chinese. Although highly concise and fixed in form, they can usually convey profound meanings vividly. Most idioms are derived from ancient Chinese literary works and are usually related to some myths, legends or historical events. It is difficult to understand the exact meaning of an idiom without the knowledge of its origin. Therefore, learning idioms helps people better understand Chinese traditional culture. Idioms are widely used in daily conversation and literary creation. Proper use of idioms can make one's language more expressive and communication more

effective.

8. At present, the Chinese language is used as a native language by the greatest number of people in the world. One of the significant distinctions between the Chinese and the Western languages lies in the fact that it is composed of characters rather than letters. The Chinese language is the oldest writing system still in use today. Although people from different regions in China may not understand each other's dialects, they have little difficulty in communication because Chinese characters are written in a uniform way. The Chinese language has played quite an important role in the unification of the Chinese nation in history. Nowadays, with China's rapid economic growth and increasing global influence, more and more people in other countries begin to learn Chinese.

9. In recent years, more and more museums in China have been open to the public free of charge. The number of museum exhibitions and visitors to museums have seen an obvious increase. It has become very common to see that people stand in long queues in front of some popular museums. Therefore, these museums must take measures to restrict the number of visitors. Nowadays, the forms of exhibitions become increasingly diverse. Some large museums use advanced technologies such as multimedia and virtual reality to make their exhibitions more attractive. Quite a few museums also hold online exhibitions where people can enjoy the sight of rare and precious exhibits. However, the experience of viewing the exhibits on site is still more appealing to most visitors.

10. Innovation is progressing at an unprecedented speed in China. In order to catch up with those developed nations in science and technology as fast as possible, China has substantially invested more funds for development research in recent years. Universities and research institutions in China are actively carrying out innovation researches, covering a number of high-tech fields such as big data, biochemistry, new energy and robots, etc. They also cooperate with science parks in various regions, commercializing the achievements of innovation. Meanwhile, no matter in production or business model, entrepreneurs in China are competing to be pioneers in innovation to adapt to the constantly changing and increasing needs of the consumer market at home and abroad.

附录3 全国研究生入学考试翻译考题指南及真题演练

参考译文

1. (1) 战争结束后,这些西方社会的高等教育的入学率水平不一,而战争爆发前的几十年间,这些社会的入学率大致保持在相关年龄群体的3%~5%。

   (2) 在那些社会,人们对接受高等教育的需求不断上升,而且战前没有想过上大学的群体和社会阶层也产生了这种需求。

   (3) 在西欧许多国家,高等教育的学生人数在20世纪60年代的五年内翻了一番,到70年代中期,高等教育学生人数又在7年、8年或10年内翻了一番。

   (4) 如果新入职的员工主要都是研究生刚毕业的年轻男女教师,他们在很大程度上决定了该学院的学术活动规范。

   (5) 高等教育的快速发展增加了学术创新的机会,同时也削弱了教师和学生在先前高等教育稳定而缓慢的增长时期加入学者群体的形式和过程。

2. (1) 由于文艺复兴时期教会倡导的教义和思维方式逐渐黯然失色,中世纪和现代之间的差距得以弥合,从而开启了等待人们探索的全新知识领域。

   (2) 在这些科学家们公布他们伟大的发现之前,当时许多思想家都继续采用更为古老的思维方式,包括托勒密和亚里士多德提出的地心说,即认为地球是我们宇宙的中心。

   (3) 尽管教会努力打压新一代的逻辑学家和理性学者的观点,但是关于宇宙运行方式的新学说层出不穷,发展态势之迅猛以至于不容忽视,包括教会神职人员也开始被迫接受这些观点。

   (4) 正是由于很多人致力于尝试用推理和科学哲理的方式探索这个世界,文艺复兴时代结束了,一个全新的理性的时代到来了。

   (5) 这些探寻新知识以及彻底挖掘理解已知信息的努力尝试可以用一个拉丁文短语来描述,那就是"敢于探索"。

3. (1) 医学期刊中存在大量此类无稽之谈,经广播公司和新闻媒体报道,则会引发人们对健康问题的恐慌并激起短暂的食疗热潮。

   (2) 如今的研究岗位需要申请者发表的论文数量,是十年前同一岗位所需论文量的两倍。

   (3) 为遏制这种趋势,人们已做出了一些尝试,例如在评估申请者论文的过程中纳入质量和数量双重标准。

   (4) 如果科学家没有在未来的出版物中轻易引用自己的论文,也没有指使同事为其这样去做以换取类似的好处,那么该索引评估便是合理的。

   (5) 若想严格确保科学既有意义又可再生,我们还必须确保我们的体制支持发展这种科学才行。

4. (1) 莎士比亚出生之时,盛极近五个世纪的宗教戏剧在欧洲逐渐走向没落,在古典悲剧和喜剧的激发下,很多新兴的混合式戏剧形式应运而生。

(2) 任何文法学校的学生都知道戏剧是文学的一种形式,它曾给古希腊和古罗马带来荣耀,也许同样会给英格兰带来殊荣。

(3) 但是,专业戏剧公司在固定的剧院中繁荣发展起来,吸引高等学府中有文学抱负的人迅速投身这些剧院,并为他们解决生计问题。

(4) 一种本土文学戏剧诞生了,这一艺术形式与公共剧院结成联盟,一些伟大的戏剧传统也逐渐显现并开始登上历史舞台。

(5) 为了真正了解当时的戏剧性活动有多么繁盛,我们必须铭记这些事实:大量剧本都已经丢失了,并且几乎没有哪位知名作家的所有作品都保留了下来。

5. (1) 但是,尽管说英语的人数还在进一步增加,有迹象表明,在可预见的未来英语可能会逐渐丧失其全球主导地位。

(2) 有些人认为,英语的全球地位无懈可击,英国的年轻一代甚至无需学习其他语言技能。因此,大卫的分析可能会给这部分人的骄傲自大画上一个句号。

(3) 众多国家正在将英语纳入小学课程体系,而英国却似乎没有加大力度鼓舞学龄儿童和其他学生熟练掌握其他语言。

(4) 大卫·格兰多指出的这些变化显然给英国一些教授他国人士英语的教育机构以及更广大的教育行业都带来了巨大的挑战。

(5) 这给所有致力于推广英语学习和应用的机构提供了一个依据,使其能够在此基础上制定规划,更好地应对一个迥然不同的运营环境所带来的各种可能性。

6. (1) 我们无需刻意去学习怎样才能保持心理健康;正如我们的身体知道怎样愈合伤口和修复骨折一样,保持心理健康是我们与生俱来的能力。

(2) 我们的心理健康并非真的消失不见了;就像云朵背后的太阳,或许暂时被遮挡,但是它可以在瞬间重焕光芒。

(3) 心理健康使我们在他人遇到麻烦时给予同情,在他人痛苦时心存善意,而且无论对方是谁都会给予无条件的关爱。

(4) 尽管拥有健康的心智是我们生活中的万能药,但它并不稀奇,你会发现每当面对艰难的抉择,它一直在指引着你。

(5) 你会慢慢领悟,明白健康的心智一直陪伴我们左右,是一位值得信赖的朋友,那么此刻我们就可以放缓生活节奏,尽情享受生活。

7. (1) 在多种强大动机的驱使下,这场移民潮在一片荒野上建起了一个国家,并且从本质上塑造了这片处女地的性格和命运。

(2) 美国正是两种主导力量交织互动的产物——拥有不同思想、风俗和民族特征的欧洲移民,以及一个崭新的国家重新整合这些特性所带来的影响。

(3) 但由于美国独特的地理条件,不同民族相互影响,以及在一片未开化的新大陆难以维持欧洲所有的老惯例,众多显著的变化正在酝酿之中。

(4) 15 至 16 世纪,人们远洋探险,发现了北美新大陆;一百多年后,第一批移民横渡大西洋,来到这片土地——今日的美国。

(5) 广袤无垠的原始森林从缅因州一路绵延到乔治亚州,拥有大量种类繁多的树木,堪称一大宝藏。

8. (1) 这也是为什么当我们试图用语言来描述音乐时,我们只能表达自己对于音乐的感受,而无法领悟音乐本身。

(2) 人们普遍认为,贝多芬是个思想自由、充满勇气的人。我发现勇气这一品质是理解贝多芬音乐作品的关键,演奏他的作品自然更是如此。

(3) 贝多芬习惯用极其强烈的力度来提乐曲的音量,然后又出乎意料地突然跟上一个轻柔的乐段。之前的作曲家极少采用这种作曲方式。

(4) 尤为重要的是贝多芬对于自由的看法,他认为自由事关每个人的权利和责任:他倡导思想自由和个人言论自由。

(5) 我们可以这样解释贝多芬的大部分作品:苦难是不可避免的,但是与痛苦抗争的勇气造就了值得勇往直前的精彩人生。

9. (1) 然而,那些无家可归者所创造的花园尽管风格多样,却超越了装饰美化或创造性表达的需求,道出了其他各种基本诉求。当我们看到这些照片,便会感受到一种深深的震撼。

(2) 一方神圣的净土,不管它多么简陋,都是人类不可缺少的。它跟巢穴截然不同,后者只是满足了动物的栖身需求。

(3) 无家可归者描绘的花园实质上是无所依附的,这些花园把一种形式引入城市环境之中,而这种形式要么根本不存在,要么表现为一种隐性的存在方式,难以识别。

(4) 我们大多数人会深陷于精神萎靡的状态,并常常将此归咎为一些心理原因,直到有一天我们发现自己置身花园之中,感到那些压抑和烦闷如魔法般烟消云散。

(5) 正是这种与大自然之间或含蓄或直白的联系,充分证实了从"广义"角度使用"花园"这个词来描述这些人造建筑是合乎情理的。

10. (1) 物理学中的一个理论把这种归一的冲动发挥到了极致,探寻一种万有理,即为我们所见之物寻求一种单一的生成公式。

(2) 在此,达尔文主义似乎提供了合理的解释,假如全人类起源于共同的祖先,那么就有理由认为,文化多样性同样也可以追溯到数量有限的几个文化原型。

(3) 从共性中提炼出独特性,也许能让我们明白文化行为起源的复杂性,以及文化行为在进化或认知过程中的源动力。

(4) 第二个为此做出努力的人是约书亚·格林伯格。他采用实证主义的方法来研究普遍性,证实了多种语言(尤其是语序方面)的共同特征,这些特征被认为代表了由认知局限导致的偏差。

(5) 乔姆斯基的生成语法表明语言变化的模式,这些模式独立于族谱或贯穿其中的路径,然而格林伯格的共性理论预见了特定类型的语序关系中存在强烈的相互依存性。

附录4 口译加油站

1 礼仪接待
原文：

A：Excuse me. Are you Mr. Miller from Eastern Electronics?

B：Yes, I am. And you must be Ms.Zheng, right?

A：Yeah, you are right. Welcome to Shanghai! I am here to pick you up.

B：Nice to see you. Thanks for meeting me at the airport in person!

A：My pleasure. I'm delighted to meet you, too. How was the trip?

B：Not bad.

A：I've heard so much about you from Mr. Liu.

B：I've been looking forward to visiting your country, and now here I am.

A：The more you know about our country, the more you'll like it. I do wish you a pleasant stay here.

B：I'm expecting.

A：Mr. Liu is having an important meeting at the moment. He'll come to see you later at the hotel. Please give me your luggage check, and I'll get them for you.

B：Thank you, here youare. I'm sure I can count on you for help during my stay here.

A：You are welcome.

答案：
1.E 2.A 3.I 4.G 5.J 6.B 7.F 8.C

2 商务交流
原文：

A：Do you mean to say that if we cntrust you with the agency, you will sell $1,000,000 each year?

B：I couldn't have said it any better. But we expect a 10% commission, of course.

A：Our agents in other areas usually get a 5%～7% commission.

B：But your product is still new to our market, and we need to do a lot of work and spend a lot of money on sales promotion.

A：A 10% commission won't leave us much. As you know, we are a well-established firm in the line of textiles, and we enjoy good relations with all the wholesalers, chain stores and distributors in Canada.

B：You'll later find it most worthwhile if you appoint us as your sole agent.

A: Thank you for your intention to help promote the sales of our products, and we are quite satisfied with your performance in the last two years. But honestly, an annual sales volume of ＄1,000,000 does not justify a sole agency agreement.

B: If we are granted the sole agency, we can assure you that we'll double the turnover.

A: OK, we'd be willing to bend the rules a little. We agree to offer a 10% commission.

B: Then that's settled.

答案:
1. B 2. G 3. D 4. F 5. J 6. I 7. A 8. E

3 叙述介绍

原文:

  Seasonal affective disorder (SAD), also referred to as winter disorder, is a type of depression that sets in or starts in the winter months. Unlike other types of depression, it is often a cyclical, recurring disorder — you'll feel depression every winter and begin to feel better each spring. SAD depression is caused by lowered levels of serotonin, the mood-affecting brain chemical that is triggered by seasonal changes in daylight. Shorter days may also disrupt the body's biological clock which upsets the balance of melatonin, the hormone which regulates mood and sleep patterns. Seasonal affective disorder is far more common in northern climates, where days can be very short in winter. SAD affects more women than men and is likelier to occur in people under age 40 than those older than that.

  Year-end panic refers to the self-reproach and overall feeling of panic brought about by the approach of the year's end, often due to a poor financial year and pressure from work and family. Psychological experts suggest that we should avoid peer competition. While regretting for the failed plans in the past year, you can still make resolution to do it better in the coming year.

答案:
1. H 2. F 3. C 4. G 5. A 6. J 7. I 8. D

4 旅游观光

原文:

  Known for its plethora of ancient ruins, whitewashed villages, sunny beaches, tasty cuisine and friendly atmosphere, Greece ranks among Europe's top travel destinations.

But the reason that tourism exists in the first place is that it's just so beautiful here. Often, you'll find that beauty on the many scattered islands, lying like little gems in the seas surrounding the Grecian peninsula. Each one offers its own share of stunning landscapes, historic sites, nightlife scenes and cultural delights.

  Situated at the southernmost tip of the Attica peninsula, Cape Sounion is best known as the site of the ruins of the ancient Greek temple of Poseidon, the god of the sea. The remains are perched on the headland, surrounded on three sides by the sea. The site is a popular day-excursion for tourists from Athens, with sunset over the Aegean Sea, as viewed from the ruins, a sought-after spectacle.

答案：
1. C 2. H 3. G 4. I 5. F 6. J 7. B 8. E

5 论证演说
原文：
  Since the end of the Cold War, the overall tension around the world tends to ease off. There has been an increasingly louder call for peace, stability and development from people of the world. China expressed strong indignation at Japanese Prime Minister Koisumi's visit to the Yasukuni Shrine. The shrine honors Class-A war criminals whose hands were stained with the blood of the people of China and other Asian countries. His shrine visit impaired the political basis of Sino-Japanese relations. The Chinese people cannot accept such actions by a Japanese leader. Taking history as a mirror and looking forward to the future is the only right attitude to historical issues. One has to have a sense of right and wrong. Without it, a person cannot be trusted, and a country cannot hold its own in the family of nations.

答案：
1. D 2. F 3. G 4. B 5. J 6. A 7. H 8. I

6 融会贯通
原文：
  Tech giants Apple and Google are teaming up to create a system that would let smartphone users know when they've come into contact with someone who has COVID-19. The technology would rely on the Bluetooth signals that smartphones can both send out and receive. If a person tests positive for COVID-19, he could notify public health

authorities through an app. Those public health apps would then alert anyone whose smartphones had come near the infected person's phone in the prior 14 days. The technology could be used on both Google Android phones and Apple iPhones. The companies insist that they will preserve smartphone users' privacy. Smartphone users must opt in to use it. The software will not collect data on users' physical locations or their personally identifiable information. People who test positive would remain anonymous, both to the people who come in contact with them and to Apple and Google.

答案：
1. D 2. A 3. E 4. I 5. G 6. B 7. H 8. F